Brighton

History and Guide

Brighton's world famous seafront in mid-Victorian days (seen from the West Pier)

Brighton
History and Guide

Mark Sampson

ALAN SUTTON PUBLISHING LIMITED

First published in the United Kingdom in 1994
Alan Sutton Publishing Limited
Phoenix Mill · Far Thrupp · Stroud · Gloucestershire

First published in the United States of America in 1994
Alan Sutton Publishing Inc. · 83 Washington Street · NH 03820

British Library Cataloguing in Publication Data

A catalogue record for this book is available from the British Library.

ISBN 0–7509–0476–3

Jacket Illustration: Brighton Pavilion.

Typeset in 10/13 Times.
Typesetting and origination by
Alan Sutton Publishing Limited.
Printed in Great Britain by
Ebenezer Baylis, Worcester.

Contents

For my grandfather,
Leslie Sampson,
a gentleman and a wonder to us all

Preface

According to Councillor Peter Martin, the mayor of Hove, people settle and stay in his borough. As for Brighton, 'people don't stay there for very long and most of the people who do weren't actually born there'.

By this criterion, I would claim to be fairly representative. Born in London and reared in Belfast, I moved to Brighton in 1977 to take an MA in American Studies at Sussex University. I fell in love with the town and stayed for ten years. That's long enough, perhaps, to qualify for citizenship.

Then I moved on. Living now in Sheffield, I am conscious of questions being raised in the house: 'What credentials does *he* have for writing this book?' I can only suggest that anyone who has ever lived in Brighton, maybe ever *visited* Brighton, will never get the place out of their system. I still feel an affinity with and an affection for the town. What's more, I would suggest that a distance of two hundred and fifty miles and an absence of six years have revealed a healthy perspective. Perhaps, as a result, I can be more objective about the constant changes which have taken place.

As for the book itself, I haven't tried to write a definitive history. There are other, more scholarly books on the market, and anyone wanting to explore the whole truth about Brighton need go no further than Timothy Carder's wonderful *Encyclopaedia*.

What I *have* tried to do is write an entertaining story of the town's birth and growing pains and maturity into one of the marvels of Britain. I hope it will whet the appetite and prompt further research. And I hope that the two walks I offer at the end will help you carry out some of that research on foot. Brighton, I believe, is its very own museum and art gallery.

Brighton's growth (showing main road and rail arteries)

CHAPTER ONE

Queen of the South

'It gets you and that's it.'
'I can't think of anywhere else I'd rather be.'

Saturday morning market traders, 1993

Hail guest, we ask not what thou art. If friend we greet thee
hand and heart. If stranger such no longer be. If foe our love
shall conquer thee.

Inscription on the Brighton boundary pylon, A23

One of my most abiding memories of Brighton is that of stepping off the London train after a hot, sticky day in the capital: making my way across the foyer to the taxi rank outside, where a blast of pure ozone restores me to life. The breeze blows straight up West Street and Queen's Road, direct from the sea front, cool as a mint and rich with the tang of brine and malt vinegar.

At such times, it's like being a child again, arriving at the seaside. And, after all, Brighton is, first and foremost, a seaside resort. If not the first in the country – residents of Scarborough may debate that issue – it is certainly the largest. The 1991 census records a population of 154,200. The conurbation which centres around Brighton, and which extends from Saltdean in the east to Shoreham in the west, is one of the twenty or so largest in England and Wales. More overseas visitors stay in Brighton than in any other town outside London, and with nearly seven hundred thousand staying visitors each year and a further two million day-trippers, the livelihoods of 11 per cent of the town's working population are directly linked to the tourist industry. Those of many more are linked indirectly.

Writing in 1850, Edwin Lee described Brighton as being 'situate at the bottom of a bay, formed to the east by Beachy Head, and by Worthing Point on the west; built on a rising hill, having a south-eastern exposition, and defended on the north'. That natural defence

Brighton rock – seven sticks a pound

takes the form of the South Downs, whose solid chalk meets the sea at Black Rock in the first of a series of spectacular white cliffs which stretch to Newhaven and Beachy Head beyond.

The proximity of the Downs helps to lure people to Brighton. It also helps to account for the distinctive look of the town. Given the natural chalk amphitheatre to the north and the east, and the demand for sea peeps and bella vistas, the resort first spread eastwards and westwards from the Old Town at its core. Its majestic, elongated sea front is elevated on cliffs of chalk rubble and flint which tail off gradually from Kemp Town towards Hove and a floor of clay and sand to the west.

Two steep-sided combes or valleys, marked broadly by the Lewes and London Roads of today, separate three spurs of the Downs which reach down towards the sea. These combes meet in the broad valley which denotes the original heart of the town (and the focus of modern-day traffic). Here, the lost River Wellesbourne once flowed. Ever since it was diverted into a sewer culvert at the end of the eighteenth century, Brighton has become that rare phenomenon: a town without a river.

As the town boundaries and its population have expanded, so the suburbs have pushed inland: along the two combes, and higher and higher up the steep spurs. Should you fail to notice it from the train, your legs will soon verify that Brighton is a remarkably hilly place.

Now, lest residents of the level boulevards of Hove should think I am using the adjective 'hilly' too freely, it would be as well to define what is meant by 'Brighton'. Despite the lack of any distinct boundaries, and despite a number of attempts to annex it, Hove is a separate borough and, for the purpose and duration of this book, shall remain so. However, because it was once a separate estate originally considered a part of Brighton, it is historically convenient if the focus of the book extends to the Brunswick area in the west – and as far as Rottingdean and Saltdean in the east. Its northern boundary is formed, roughly, by the new by-pass.

For years there has been a keen, though generally good-natured rivalry between Brighton and Hove. Indeed, recently the mayor of Hove complained of the 'years of taking a back seat' to its arrogant neighbour. Perhaps Brighton can be so accused – if confidence in its own appeal is synonymous with arrogance. But Hove, too, is aware of its charm. As a notice in Brunswick Square proclaims, the borough 'retains its reputation as a distinguished resort with a more peaceful atmosphere than Brighton'. In order to define, with any satisfaction, Brighton's unique spirit of place, the contrast is a useful one.

So, peaceful it is not. What is it, therefore, that brings so many visitors to Brighton? Is it simply the combination of sea and South Downs? In addition to the celebrated sea front, a 1920 guidebook cites its nearness to London, a splendid railway service, its proximity to the continent, invigorating air, 'perfect sanitary conditions' and 'a water supply above suspicion'. Most of this holds true today. Then there are the twin piers, the Pavilion and other architectural gems; the fascinating shops of the Lanes and the North Laine area; two hundred restaurants and a host of golden entertainment facilities; and a climate which boasts over one thousand seven hundred hours of sunshine and less than 30 in of rain per year. (Richard Jeffries may have been a little fanciful when he described Brighton in 1885 as 'a Spanish town in England, a Seville', but the town certainly boasts better weather than, say, Manchester.)

No wonder, then, that Lydia Bennett in *Pride and Prejudice* talks of a visit to Brighton comprising 'every possibility of earthly happiness'. And though her thoughts were more focused on young men in uniform, it is surely true that the spirit of the place resides somewhere in the sheer wealth and range of its attractions. Indeed, any attempt to distil them into a single essence is probably as doomed as the 'Spirit of Brighton' statue: the unfortunate, unloved orphan of the post-war planners, which became a sanitary facility for the pigeons of Churchill Square until its recent – and merciful – removal.

Someone described Brighton, succinctly, as 'a 365-day-of-the-year town'. The various, more familiar epithets given to the town in its time – the social capital of England, the queen of watering places, London-by-the-Sea – reflect not only a rich history, but also this chameleon-like ability to provide all things to all people. 'Something for everyone' is not just a glib slogan.

Less than 50 miles due south of the capital, Brighton is the nearest south coast resort to London. While the legions of commuters head north during the week, on weekends and public holidays the exodus is reversed. Many day-trippers are refugees from the metropolis, and many come primarily for the sea and shingle. On the other hand, weekenders, holidaymakers and conference delegates will be more likely to discover the markets, the specialist shops, the bars and bistros and fringe entertainments of Bohemian Brighton. It is, as the current guidebook suggests, a 'colourful cosmopolitan blend of culture and candyfloss'.

'Cosmopolitan' is a useful adjective. Brighton is a melting pot, and all around there is evidence of visitors, past and present. Yet there is still more to this spirit of place than its multifarious quality. Another look at some of the ingredients outlined above will reveal one more – and sometimes overlooked – spirit. And that is the spirit of paradox.

That Brighton once rivalled Bath as a centre of the beau monde is quite evident in the number of monuments to great architects, such as Nash, Barry, Waterhouse and the local heroes, Busby and the Wilds (both father and son): it is said that Brighton has more listed buildings than any other town in Britain. However, the stuccoed buildings which dominate the sea front are like gleaming white teeth

The Peace Memorial marking
the Brighton–Hove border, and
the 'gleaming white teeth' of
the Brunswick sea front

which, on closer inspection, reveal the need for some major root-
canal work. Today, the great houses are partitioned into flats and
sub-divided into bedsits. Though a recent report attributed the best
life-style in Britain to Brighton, housing problems and poverty are
rife: the *Evening Argus* of 20 July 1993 reported 'the highest
percentage of homeless people in the country'.

Anyone who has seen or read Graham Greene's *Brighton Rock*
will know of Brighton's supposed seedy underbelly. Today, the
labels 'dirty weekend' and 'kiss-me-quick' may be rather tired, but it
is undeniable that the place still has a raffish charm which helps to
humanize the grandeur.

Much of this raffish charm is associated with the patronage of a
lovable rogue who made the grade from philandering prince to king
of the realm. As prince regent, George IV was the figurehead of the
Whigs; for most of the nineteenth century, his favourite town
returned mainly Liberal MPs. Nevertheless, as the prime town of
Sussex, a Tory stronghold, Brighton has returned virtually all
Conservative MPs since the 1880s. When Dennis Hobden took Kemp
Town in 1964, it became the only Sussex seat ever won by Labour.

One of the abiding features of Brighton life is its remarkable
tolerance. George IV patronized the arts and helped transform Brighton
into the kind of Bohemian town which could accommodate his Pavilion
– and its variations on a theme. The town has a strong theatrical
tradition; in post-war years, Lord Olivier and Dame Flora Robson
almost came to be regarded as Brighton's unofficial monarchy. Edward
Burne-Jones and Rudyard Kipling lived and worked in Rottingdean.
Charles Dickens wrote *Dombey and Son* at the Bedford Hotel, and gave

Variations on a royal theme

readings at the town hall. Thackeray wrote much of *Vanity Fair* in Brighton. Others linked to the town include Aubrey Beardsley, Eric Gill, Arnold Bennett, Lewis Carroll and Terence Rattigan. Brighton's eccentrics have been celebrated locally and nationally; the great Max Miller, Magnus Volk, the inventor, and Gavin Henderson, the current director of the Brighton Festival, spring readily to mind.

The Royal Pavilion is, of course, unique (though its ostentatious artificiality smacks of the residential wedding cakes of Beverly Hills). The Hollywood analogy is not as fanciful as it might sound: William Friese-Greene, the first person to put a moving picture on celluloid, and a whole school of other pioneers of the cinema lived and worked around Brighton. And film-makers could do worse than mine the rich seam of legend and folklore attached to the town: the walled-up nun of the Lanes, Lady Elena and the Ghost Ship, the escape of Charles II, the smugglers of Rottingdean, the Constance Kent affair and much more.

The tolerance extends to religion. Dissenters have always found a place of worship in Brighton (though Deryk Carver paid for his beliefs by becoming the first Protestant martyr in Queen Mary's reign). Indeed, the links with Cardinal Newman and the Oxford Movement in Victorian times fed a form of High Church ceremony which was labelled as the 'London, Brighton and South Coast religion'. Its 'high priest', the Revd Arthur Wagner, is also known as one of Brighton's renowned champions of the people. Interestingly, an early co-operative movement flowered here some years before its official birth in Rochdale.

Other municipal claims suggest a ready acceptance of change which must go hand-in-hand with all this tolerance. The town can

The West Pier: listed and adrift

probably boast the oldest continuous public electricity supply in the world. Volk's railway was the first public electric railway in Britain. Today the Marina is one of the largest man-made harbours in the world. Personally, I rather like the fact that Brighton has the largest municipal rock garden in England. And how suitably ironic that the ruined West Pier is the only Grade I listed pier in Britain.

My point, though, is that nothing ever stands still in the town. Successive visits reveal always an invigorating blend of familiarity and surprise. In my time I witnessed the last years of Beall & Co.'s cork shop and the first, humble years of the Body Shop empire. These days it is apparent how the town can accommodate a large gay population along with all its older, more traditional residents – and all those visitors.

When I asked someone why he moved to Brighton, he replied that he used to live in Crawley. Without being unkind to Crawley, I knew exactly what he meant. Brighton has no single, abiding characteristic. Whereas one might link Bath, say, with Georgian architecture, Salisbury with its cathedral, Oxford with its university, Sheffield with steel, Brighton's unique selling point (in marketing parlance) is its very 'Brightonness'. Finally, the charm of the place lies in its blend of antitheses: old and new; rich and poor; grandeur and squalor. Somewhere among its diversity, variety, ironies and paradoxes, its 'consistent unpredictability', reside the spirits of place.

Harry Preston, the great impresario, described his town as the 'Queen of the South'. The phrase is redolent of Brighton's regal past and its camp theatricality. It might also conjure up an obscure brand of real ale. In the forthcoming chapters of this book, I shall trace the town's development from a small fishing community to a major resort and examine the origins of all the ingredients which constitute the rare, intoxicating brew that is Brighton.

The intoxicating high spirits of the place

CHAPTER TWO

From Creation . . .

If, according to some antiquaries, Brighthelmston had a Roman origin, it must have continued in a state below mediocrity since scarcely any mention is made of the town by our oldest historians.

from *The Stranger in Brighton* (1824)

Brighton has another strange claim to fame. The racecourse is the only one in Britain owned and run by a local authority. 'In forming the new Race Ground at the beginning of 1822,' the unidentified author of *The Stranger in Brighton* wrote, 'the workmen had occasion to cut through several of the tumuli inclosed within the intrenchments of White-hawk hill.' Some hundred and sixty years later, bulldozers extending the Freshfield estate came within yards of ploughing through a scheduled ancient monument: the same earliest-known inhabited site in Brighton.

Whitehawk hill camp is one of twelve known Neolithic 'causewayed' camps, so called because the concentric banks and ditches, which enclose the central area, are interrupted by numerous causeways – apparently to allow access to the centre. Built on top of Whitehawk hill, nearly 400 ft above sea level, the camp is today partly covered by the pulling-up ground of the racecourse. Little visual evidence remains, but we know that it dates back to around 3000 BC, encloses 12 acres of land and measures some 950 ft north to south and 700 ft east to west. Though its prominent site suggests some kind of fortification or statement of power, it is more probable that camps such as this were used as meeting places for members of the tribe, who would live and work nearby, but assemble for festivals or meetings, or at times of danger.

Certainly such excavated items as decorated pots, flint tools, fireplaces and bones suggest human concourse. Evidence of cattle slaughter might link the camp with some kind of ritualistic or ceremonial function and the charred human bones found indicate that the inhabitants may have been cannibals.

The well-preserved skeletons of a young woman and her baby, displayed in Brighton museum, suggest a race of very small people with narrow heads. It is likely that these Neolithic settlers were immigrants from the continent who brought with them some basic techniques of agriculture. We know that they kept cattle, sheep and

The museum's Neolithic
skeleton

pigs. We know, too, that they cultivated grain, living on the hills and moving around, clearing new land as they exhausted the old. They settled particularly densely in Sussex, because the soil on the chalk Downs was light, well drained and easily cleared. Though the soil was poorer on top, the valleys were wetter, more wooded and, therefore, harder to clear. The Sussex Downs are also rich in the flint which provided the raw materials for their tools and, a few thousand years later, for many of the houses built in what was to become Brighton.

The next wave of European immigrants to settle in Britain introduced the science of copper metallurgy; their discovery that the addition of 10 per cent tin to copper produced a more durable alloy, more suitable for heavy-duty tools (and weapons) than flint, lent the name 'Bronze Age' to the next major phase of pre-history. That they settled alongside the indigenous farming population in the Brighton area (as elsewhere in England) is borne out by the number of barrows, or burial mounds, discovered in, for example, Patcham, Stanmer Woods, Ditchling Road and the Surrenden Road area.

Had it not been for the treasure-seekers and amateur archaeologists of the eighteenth and nineteenth centuries, there might have been more evidence of this civilization. Fortunately, they missed the numerous bracelets or charms known as 'The Brighton Loops', and they missed the greatest treasure of all from this period – the Amber Cup, found in 1856 on the site of a Bronze Age chieftain's barrow in Palmeira Avenue, Hove.

Ironically, the destruction wrought in the name of Brighton's new by-pass has helped archaeologists piece together evidence of the largest site of late Bronze Age huts in the county, found in the Coldean valley. The number and concentration of hut platforms found could suggest a whole village of subsistence farmers. Certainly by this time farming was a more settled activity, with cereals produced on a more systematic basis in neat, square fields – the first evidence of ox-drawn ploughs. The field systems of these and subsequent Celtic settlers can still be seen all over the Downs. Of course, many have been destroyed by subsequent agriculture and development, but if you look west from the Sunblest factory in Lower Bevendean you can clearly see the lynchets, or banks, which formed as a result of soil slip from ploughing, at the lower edge of the field.

There is another municipal attraction which incorporates a scheduled ancient monument. I used to approximate golf at the Hollingbury public course, quite unaware that I was skirting an early Iron Age hill fort, dating from around the sixth century BC. Just as the hill fort found above the Devil's Dyke commands views all over the Weald, the one at Hollingbury was built on the summit of a prominent hill, nearly 600 ft above sea level. On a clear day, you can see as far as the New Forest to the west and Hastings to the east. 'Within signalling distance', surmised the *Sussex Daily News* of 1903, 'of other similar camps.'

The term 'hill fort' is generally used to describe such a hilltop site, bounded by a bank of earth and rubble, and surrounded by the ditch from which this material was quarried. E. Cecil Curwen's discovery in 1931 of two holes for gateposts revealed that the camp was guarded by a single pair of massive gates, 10 ft across.

While the economy of the times was still founded largely on agriculture, the purpose of hill forts was clearly defence. Society was probably based on local chiefdoms, with these forts marking the edge or centre of their territory and acting as a kind of community centre

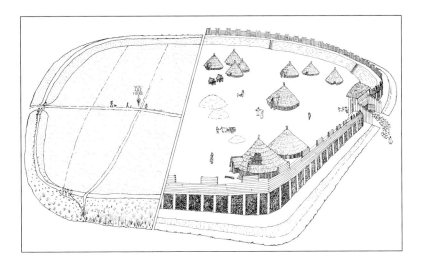

Hollingbury hill fort: now and then

for the immediate area. The remains of five round huts were found within the Hollingbury walls and it is likely that it served as a temporary place of refuge from, say, cattle rustlers, crop stealers, even the odd rampaging invader. As the population grew and land became scarcer, and the times became more troubled, these hill forts probably became more permanent, more organized places of sanctuary. However, despite the size of the Hollingbury encampment, there is no evidence to suggest that here was an embryonic town. It is disappointing to record that all these early settlers had little or no influence at all on the shape of Brighton-to-come.

Twentieth-century excavations finally dispelled the kind of misleading 'supposition of this place having been a Roman Station' typified by *The Brighthelmstone Directory* of 1770. Nevertheless, the popular myth was granted full poetic licence in the Brighton Pageant of 1951, a week-long 'Cavalcade through the Ages' staged in Preston Park. The scene of Episode One was 'a Roman Camp at Brighton. . . . It is high holiday in the Camp, which is *en fete* in celebration of the visit of Julius Caesar, who has landed at Shoreham and is now on his way to the Camp' (to watch 'chariot races in his honour')! Hundreds of years later, Brighton came to rival Bath, but the place was no Aquae Sulis in Roman times.

So what was it like? Apart from a few coins and other artefacts, there isn't much to go on. Roman villas have been excavated at Southwick, at Hangleton and West Blatchington in Hove, and on the site of the Brighton Ford garage, at the corner of Springfield Road. The number of bones and the burial urns found on the latter site created speculation that it might have been some kind of temple cum cemetery.

After the initial Roman campaigns of AD 43, Sussex became a platform for the next military excursions. The area settled down to the process of becoming just another Romanized province of the empire, with an administrative centre at Noviomagus – today's Chichester. Villas like those in the Brighton area would have formed the centre of large estates and were probably owned by Romano-Britons who grew wealthy from corn production, stock-raising and trade. While the native British peasant farmers still tended to live and work in scattered settlements over the Downs, the Brighton villas exemplify the way these estates developed on the richer soil of the coastal plain, and at the foot and southern fringes of the Downs. The water table would have been much higher then and the lost River Wellesbourne would have been easily found. Besides, with its situation on a porous bed of chalk which was to serve as a giant natural reservoir for the town, the Brighton area would have offered these landowners a good supply of water, a range of soils, and access to rivers, an emerging network of roads – and the sea.

Brighton's coat of arms
reflects the town's maritime
origins

The age of Roman rule was largely a peaceful, settled one. But the fact that later Romano-British villas were often built further in from the coast is a reflection of more troubled times: from the late third century AD onwards, pirates from the coasts of the Netherlands, Germany and Scandinavia began to raid Britain's shores. These Saxons, as they were collectively known, were just some of the many barbarian hordes, throughout the western Empire, which were stretching the imperial forces to breaking point. Effectively told to defend themselves, the Britons at first succeeded in repelling the raiding Picts, Irish and Saxons. Then, under renewed threat of invasion in AD 428, the Council of the States decided to pay Saxon mercenaries, or 'laeti', to fight for them against the invaders.

Just over a hundred years later, the Saxons held sway over much of England. Gildas, a British priest and contemporary historian, lamented the 'hopeless stupidity' of asking 'vile unspeakable Saxons' into the country. Nevertheless, the origins of Brighton as a significant settlement can be traced to these same unspeakable people. In fact, 'Sussex' means the kingdom of the South Saxons and it has been said that no district in England has a clearer Saxon ancestry.

Their influence in the Brighton area is particularly evident in the place names. Saxon words like 'ton', 'ing', 'ham', 'stan', 'mer' and 'dene' form parts of names like 'Stanmer' ('stony lake'), 'Ovingdean' ('the valley of Ofa's people'), or 'Preston' ('the priest's farmstead'). A map of the town reveals an inordinate number of 'deans': Tongdean, Coldean, Withdean, Bevendean, Hollingdean and Rottingdean. Even the name 'Brighton' is a convenient abbreviation of its older name, 'Brighthelmston', itself a probable corruption of 'Beorthelm' or 'Brithelm' (a person) and 'tun', meaning village or homestead.

So it seems that the settlement of Brighton was founded some time in the Saxon period. Initially, perhaps, just a farm, it grew up where it did because of such factors as the water supply, the convenient routes to Lewes and beyond, the large, flat sheltered area which the Steine provided for boats and again, of course, the sea. Thus, an embryonic fishing industry developed, and a fishing village probably took root on the extensive chalk foreshore below the cliff (today's esplanade), protected as it was from the full force of the Channel by an offshore submarine bar of shale.

Administratively, Brighton was then in the Hundred of Welesmere in the 'Rape of Lewes'. Originally based on areas either providing 100 warriors or consisting of 100 families, the Hundreds would convene courts at regular intervals to dispense justice and raise taxes. Here, the Saxon influence lasted right into the nineteenth century. This particular Hundred consisted of Ovingdean,

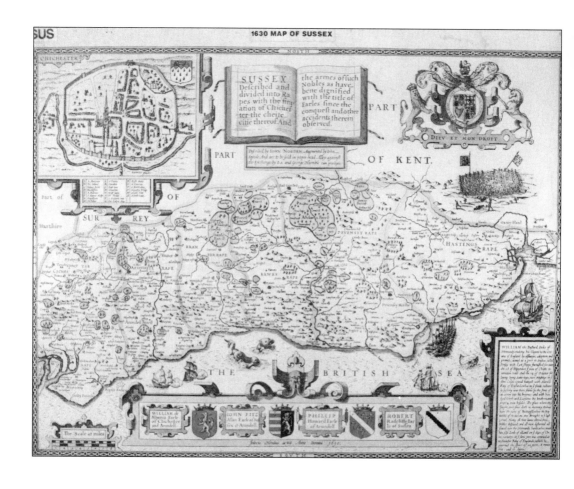

Rottingdean and Brighton itself, which was sub-divided into three manors. Two of these manors were bequeathed by Earl Godwin to his son, Harold. And everyone knows how the future King Harold II was to meet his death at nearby Hastings.

After 1066 the Normans carried out the epic inventory of all their new properties. The Domesday Book of 1086 provides the earliest documentary mention of Brighton. Sussex, we learn, was divided into six Rapes, and the Rape of Lewes, with its fifty-six manors, was granted to the mighty William de Warenne. His manors were then leased to Norman sub-tenants, and the book records that 'Bristelmestune' had three: Ralph's, Widard's and William de Watteville's. Since a tribute of four thousand herrings was paid to Ralph, it seems that the fishing industry was, by now, well established. Churches are recorded at Patcham, Preston, Ovingdean and Brighton. However, Ovingdean's delightful flint-built church of the eighth-century Saxon saint, Wulfran, appears to date from the early twelfth century; and, despite its splendid Norman font, the first parish church

Brighthelmston (just above the surfacing dolphin) in the Rape of Lewes

The Norman font in the church of St Nicholas

of Brighton, dedicated to St Nicholas of Myra (the patron saint of fishermen), would seem to date from the fourteenth century.

By piecing together the records, we can estimate a population in the region of four hundred. They would have made their livelihoods through fishing or a simple, strip-cultivation type of farming. The villagers would have lived in murky hovels built of wattle and daub, and given service and paid their dues to their local lord of the manor. Lords and villagers alike, however, all owed their allegiance to the overlord, William de Warenne. His laws make illuminating, if illogical, reading: death for anyone running away from one of his manors; fines of seven shillings and fourpence for shedding blood; and eight and fourpence for adultery.

So, to quote our commentator of 1824 again, it wasn't until Brighton was 'wrested from Harold by the Norman invader, that it acquired any importance in the annals of the county'. Though in 1086 its importance had to be measured against that of the parish of Patcham, say, whose population of between a thousand and one thousand seven hundred and fifty made it one of the largest settlements in the county.

However, in the twelfth century a small monastic chapel and priory of St Bartholomew was built near the site of the current town hall; in 1285 a high constable – the most important official of the Hundred – was appointed exclusively for Brighton; in 1301 it was named in the official list of sea ports; and, twelve years later, King Edward II granted to his 'faithful and beloved John de Warenne' a charter to hold a weekly market on Thursdays and a fair on the 'eve, day and morrow of St Bartholomew' (a flagrant piece of commercialism: among the 'rights and privileges appertaining' were those of collecting tolls and rents). Clearly then, by medieval times Brighton was rather more than a 'small village inhabited by poor fishermen'.

And so the town grew. From certain customs and names (the Black Lion that gave its name to the lane, the inn and the brewery, for example, is the Black Lion of Flanders), the suggestion is that a colony of Flemings settled in the town around the thirteenth century, and contributed to the success of the fisheries. Flax, for sails, was grown in Hove (a small fishing village first mentioned in a record of 1288), and hemp, for rope, was grown on an open area of land known as the 'Hempshares'. In later times much of the Old Town and the Lanes developed here. The equivalents of modern-day West Street and East Street, which then defined the town's lateral boundaries, were probably developed by the fishermen as their population spilled over from the 'lower town' on to the cliff top.

Between the cliff top and the hill on which St Nicholas's church was built, the medieval 'upper town' developed in a regular, rectangular street pattern, which has survived to the present day. The

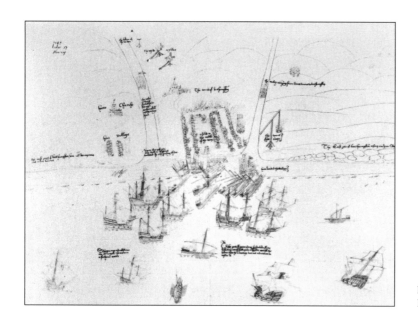

French fleet sacks medieval Brighton

northern boundary of the medieval town, today's North Street, would have been formed by the cottages and barns of the 'landsmen' who farmed the lands just to the north. Brighton's eventual topography is a legacy of the open fields system they used: the term 'laine' is a Saxon one, meaning 'loan' or 'lease' – denoting the way that the fields were leased on a piecemeal basis.

By the Middle Ages, Brighton had become part of the Hundred of 'Whalesbone' (probably a corruption of 'Wellesbourne'), which also included Hove, Patcham and West Blatchington. Its three manors were recorded as Brighthelmston-Lewes, Brighthelmston-Michelham and Brighthelmston-Atlingworth. The manors formed the basis of medieval administration and, although their powers diminished in the ages to come, their influence extended to Victorian times.

Pictorially, the best representation of the medieval town comes from a map of 1545, which depicts the 'Sacking of Brighthelmston' by the French in 1514. The ramshackle dwellings of the Lower Town, the rectangular development of the Upper Town, the elevated parish church and even neighbouring Hove are all clearly visible.

The manorial administrators had other troubles to contend with in the years leading up to this momentous raid. The first was the Black Death of 1348–50 (tradition has it that a corner of St Nicholas's churchyard was once a plague pit). And there was also the Hundred Years War which raged from 1338 to 1452. This had to be paid for, of course. Edward III levied the Nonae Tax in 1340, claiming every ninth fleece, lamb and sheaf of corn to pay for his professional

St Margaret's, Rottingdean: an American wanted to buy it

soldiers. From the appeal made by the parish to the king's tax commissioners on the grounds of poverty, crop failure and such assorted miseries as '100 acres of arable land lying annihilated by the rabbits of My Lord the Earl de Warrenne', it is evident that the area was also suffering from incursions of the sea. The appeal records that, between 1290 and 1340, 40 acres of Brighton land, 150 acres of Hove land and 50 acres of arable land around Rottingdean were 'lost, destroyed and annihilated by the violence of the sea'.

The incursions of French raiders were just as violent and rather more dramatic. When Edward III died in 1377, the French took full advantage. They sacked Hastings, Winchelsea and Rye, and landed at Rottingdean Gap in order to march on Lewes. By way of diversion, the village was plundered and set on fire. The women, children and old men who took refuge in the belfry of St Margaret's church were burned alive. To this day, some of the pillars and the western tower arch display a pinkish-red discoloration from the heat.

Even after the end of the war, hostilities kept flaring up. In a fisherman's will of 1464, William Holt bequeathed some money to 'other pouere people at the see coost in the Counte of Sussex yat have been taken prisoners by Frenshmen'. Then, on that memorable night in June 1514 the French men-of-war came sailing towards Brighthelmston. . . .

. . . to the Verge of Extinction

White may they be, like blossom on a tree
God send thousands – one, two, three,
Some by the head, some by the tail,
God send the mackerel – never fail.

Traditional fisherman's chant

The sea is very unkind. . . it would eat up the whole town.

Daniel Defoe (1724)

Unhindered, Admiral de Pregent and his troops came ashore that night in 1514, and, as Edward Hall's *Chronicle* of 1542 reports, 'he set fire to the town and took such poor goods as he found'. Finally the watch fired the beacon. As the town's defence rallied, so de Pregent sounded the retreat. In the ensuing mêlée, de Pregent 'was shot in the face with an arrow and was like to have died. And therefore he offered his image of wax before our Lady at Boulogne with the English arrow in the face, for a miracle.'

Whether that miracle transpired, we will never know. We do know that Brighton's medieval town was, with the merciful exception of St Nicholas's church, completely destroyed. We know, too, that there were bloody reprisals. As Hall's *Chronicle* records, a fleet commanded by the aptly-named Sir John Wallop, sailed to Normandy and 'burned one and twenty villages and towns with great slaughter of the people'.

So Brighton was effectively erased from the map. Nevertheless, the next phase of its history tells a remarkable story of rebirth and prosperity, followed by a long decline . . . perhaps to the very verge of extinction. By the mid-1600s Brighton was the biggest town in Sussex. Less than a hundred years later, the *Magna Britannia* survey talked of 'the inhabitants being already diminished one third less than they were, and those that remain are many of them widows,

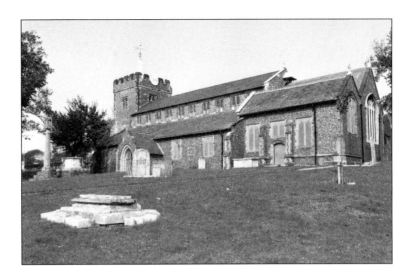

Spared – the parish church of Brighthelmston

orphans, decrepid persons and all very poor'. One constant factor helps to solve such an extraordinary, erratic equation: the sea.

In the first instance, it was the fishing industry which restored the town to its former station. Thanks to a remarkable document, preserved by Brighton's oldest firm of solicitors, we know that, by Elizabethan times, the fishing fleet of eighty vessels was probably the largest on the south coast. It records four hundred able mariners and ten thousand 'nets and lines used in their mystery', and documents the seasonal long sea voyages or 'fares' – to Scarborough between June and September for cod, and to Yarmouth between September and November for herring, as well as the shorter Channel voyages, and the local 'inshore' fares for plaice, mackerel, conger eels and herring.

On such a sound economic base, the town quickly grew up again, much as before: the Lower Town, a ramshackle collection of cottages, workshops, boats and capstans on the foreshore below the cliff, perhaps a little like what is left of the fishermen's community on the shingle at Hastings; the Upper Town laid out as per the geometric medieval street plans, and bounded by East, West and North Streets and the edge of the cliff. Access from the Lower to Upper Town was by means of a series of steep 'gaps' or clefts in the cliff, up which the cargoes landed on the beach would have been transported.

Though the majority of the extant buildings in today's Old Town date from the late eighteenth and nineteenth centuries, there are still clues as to the aspect of the reborn town. The Old Steine is now an oasis of greenery among the traffic. The word 'steine' probably derives from the Flemish word 'staene' or place of stones. In olden days, this place of stones would have provided the fishermen with some flat land for drying out their nets. And in times of bad weather, they could haul their boats on to the Steine by way of the 'Poole': the Pool Valley, or place of buses, of modern Brighton.

The town well was located on a raised area, known then as The Knab and now as Brighton Place. It is likely that this area of 'rising ground' would have served as a kind of open-air social centre for the fishing community. Though the land to the far side of North Street was still leased by their neighbours, the 'landsmen', for cultivation of corn, redevelopment of the central part of the town was encroaching on the Hempshares. The labyrinthine streets which now teem with tourists – the celebrated Lanes (probably a corruption of 'lines', as in the fishermen's lines, which would have hung from the windows of their diminutive dwellings) – date from around the late sixteenth and early seventeenth centuries, though contemporary properties may well be rebuilt or refronted versions of the originals.

The labyrinthine Lanes

The principal thoroughfares of this central area would have been linked by a network of 'twittens', a Sussex word meaning narrow path between two walls. They used to provide a crossing from one side of the town to the other, avoiding North Street and the high winds of the seafront. Many of these passageways survive: Black Lion Lane, for example, or the tiny alley connecting East Street and Little East Street. Narrow they certainly are and dark, too. Believed to date from about 1563, the two listed cottages on the south side of Black Lion Lane serve as vivid reminders of the cramped, low-built dwellings which were such a feature of the town. It is little wonder that so many ghosts and legends are associated with the murky byways of the Old Town.

Of course, with the town's regeneration came the need to defend itself from any future assailants. The French fleet, for example, tried again in 1545. This time, however, 'the beacons were fired and the inhabitants thereabouts came down so thick', according to Holinshed's *Chronicle* of 1578, that the enemy 'did little hurt there'. In 1558, the town was authorized to build a gun-battery and a store for arms on a cliff-top plot of land near the bottom of Ship Street. The resulting Blockhouse was a circular fort 50 ft in diameter, made of flint walls 18 ft high and around 7 ft thick. The ammunition was stored within and prisoners were jailed in the dungeons below. The battery in front boasted four 'great iron ordnance' (cannons) from the Tower of London.

Though no evidence survives, the *Magna Britannia* describes a 'wall three foot thick' with 'many portholes for cannon'. At 15 ft high, this massive flint wall was built on the cliff for a distance of 400 ft westward from East Street and punctuated with four 'strong Gates of Free-stone'.

The fortifications succeeded in keeping enemies out. Otherwise, however, it was a case of Brighton, open town: a haven for immigrants and religious dissenters. Indeed, a religious census in

Black Lion Lane: one of the narrowest 'twittens' of the Old Town

A reconstruction of Deryk Carver's brewery

The Blockhouse kept enemies out – but someone had to pay for it

1676 recorded 1,740 Anglicans, 260 dissenters and not a single Catholic in the parish. One such Brighton dissenter became the first Protestant to be martyred during the bloody reign of Queen Mary I. Deryk Carver was a Flemish brewer who grew hops on the Hempshares. Tradition has it that he established the Black Lion Brewery and Inn in 1546. In October 1554 he was arrested at prayer on the heinous charge of reading the Bible in English. Sent to Newgate prison, he was tried by Bishop Bonner in June the following year. Carver was found guilty of heresy and sentenced to death. The annual fireworks display at Lewes commemorates his burning in a barrel outside the Star Inn on Lewes High Street. 'And because I will not deny here God's gospel and be obedient to man's laws I am', Carver declaimed, 'condemned to die.'

To return to the matter of Brighton's fortifications, someone, of course, had to pay for them. Some funds were provided by the state, but the rest had to be found by the townspeople. Effectively, this meant the fishermen. Moreover, a growing town brought growing municipal problems. There was, for example, the business of caring for the town's poor under the terms of the 1563 Poor Law. And as the old manorial courts gradually fell into decay, so the ecclesiastical parishes came to assume the additional burden of secular administration. Empowered to levy rates for poor relief and other communal expenses, the parish vestries also appointed the officers –

in the form of churchwardens and overseers of the poor – to carry out the business of the parish. The principal income at the disposal of the churchwardens came from the fishermen's traditional 'quarter share'. Since the landsmen contributed nothing, the fishing community felt they had a grievance to address.

First, however, we should clarify the nature of their grievance. When I worked in the unemployment benefit office at Brighton, I used to process the claims of share fishermen. Why 'share' fishermen, I often wondered? The fisheries were run on a co-operative basis: with no wages as such, each catch was divided into a number of 'shares'. For a six-man vessel, say, there would be ten shares: one for each member of the crew, one for the owner of the boat, one for the owner of the nets and lines, and one for the ship's master. A further one share would be sub-divided into a half share to the vicar (as a tithe), a quarter share to the churchwardens (for 'communion plate') and a further quarter share to the churchwardens (for the defence of the town). So, although the 'quarter share' in question was only a quarter of one share of each catch, nevertheless, the fishing community were effectively the sole rate-payers.

The fishermen made their marks in the Book of Ancient Customs

And so in 1579 the fishermen petitioned Queen Elizabeth I to redress the balance. The Queen's Privy Council appointed a four-man commission to investigate these grievances. 'We will and command the said fishermen', went the commissioners' brief, 'to set down in writing the ancient customs and orders concerning the making payment, and the employing of the said quarter share.' This was duly done.

The resulting 'Booke of all the Auncient Customs' details the findings of the commissioners. History comes alive as you flick through the yellowing parchment pages of a document over four hundred years old – even though the text is written in impenetrable middle English. Translated: the quarter share levy would continue, but the landsmen would pay an individually-assessed rate of between 4d and 3s 4d per year; and a new body was established to govern the town – the Society of Twelve. This would consist of the 'Ancientest, Gravest and Wisest' inhabitants, eight of whom would be fishermen and four landsmen, and would last for very nearly two hundred years.

The commissioners also specified that, henceforth, St Nicholas's church should have three churchwardens (two fishermen and one landsman), whose duties would include 'the keeping in readiness, at all times, four barrels of gunpowder, forty of round-shot and ten of chain-shot for each and every cannon'. To this day, the parish of Brighton is unusual in retaining three churchwardens.

So the ninety 'principal' inhabitants of the town gathered to sign their names (in seven cases) or make their strange rune-like marks, and 'better increase of amity and neighbourliness in Brighton'. To 'greater

'Real' fishermen on what was
once the Lower Town

increase of brotherly love', thirty-eight years later, in 1618, the Twelve
decreed that the landsmen should 'contribute a sum equal to half that
raised by the Quarter Share'. Thus, the balance was redressed.

The Victorian author of *Brighton Fishery* wrote that 'the real
fisherman, when ashore, is a most quiet, inoffensive, good-humoured
being . . . quietly smoking his pipe and looking at the beach until the
season again summons him to sea'. We know little of the character of
the 198 men listed in 1580 as substantial householders who made
their living from fishing and cargo carrying, but their names alone are
fascinating: such stout-hearted seafarers as Thomas Tuppen, John
Speed, Sydrack Lock, Daniel Whiskey, Erasmus Winter, David
Halfpenny, William Wildboare . . . and one Nicholas Tettersoll.

Could this man have been an ancestor, father perhaps, of one of
the town's earliest (and unsung) heroes? In 1651 a Nicholas
Tettersell changed the course of British history.

By then Brighton was the largest town in Sussex, a staunchly
Parliamentarian county during the English Civil War. Indeed, two of
the signatories to the death warrant of Charles I were men of Brighton.
But with another of those ironies in which Brighton seems to
specialize, it was Tettersell whose coal brig, *The Surprise*, delivered
the fugitive Charles II to safety and nine years' exile in France.

Of course, Tettersell charged for the service; he was a business man. Nevertheless, the man was risking his life: a bounty of £1,000 was placed on the king's head, and the punishment for sheltering him was death. Indeed, only two hours after setting sail, government troops were scouring the streets of Brighton for the king. And yet, in later years, Tettersell was to suffer the slings and arrows of outrageous calumny. In various sources he has been described as odious, malevolent, a zealous bigot and a 'grubby Machiavelli'. Were such epithets justified? It is true that after taking up the office of Brighton's High Constable in 1671, he was said to be dutiful in persecuting Quakers and other non-conformists. But these were the laws of the restored monarch and the evidence against Tettersell is slender.

Nicholas Tettersell: hero or 'grubby Machiavelli'?

Certain facts we *do* know for sure. Tettersell purchased the Ship Inn and in today's Old Ship Hotel, the oldest inn in town, portraits of Tettersell, his boat and his royal passenger hang on the walls of the Tettersell bar. Moreover, the great escape is celebrated every May by the hotel's yacht race to Fécamp on the Normandy coast. But it was three years after the Restoration before he was rewarded. Even then he had to sail to London in his renamed brig, *The Royal Escape*, to claim his just deserts. On Tettersell's tombstone is a touching epitaph written by his son, which testifies to a certain understandable bitterness. 'In this cold clay he hath now 'tain up his station/Who once preserved the Church, the Crown, the Nation,' but 'Since earth did not reward the worth him given/He now receives it from the King of Heaven.'

By the time Charles II granted his saviour a pension of £100 a year, Tettersell's home town was deep in the throes of a mid-life crisis. In 1601 Brighton's largest ever fleet of sixty-six boats had sailed for the Yarmouth 'fare'. Due, however, to the restrictive (and often violent) practices of the North Sea fishing communities, to disputes with the Dutch and to the frequent attacks from Spanish and Dunkirk-based pirates, the depression in Brighton's fishing industry was reflected in the 1634 petition against Charles I's tax on maritime towns. Brighton was described as 'a poore place – and only for fishing'. On dry land its inhabitants were subject to a visitation of the plague, some severe epidemics of smallpox and frequent raids by the Royal Navy's press gangs. Increasingly, its sea-going community came to desert the North Sea in favour of coastal trading – the carrying of coal in particular. After 1697 no more boats were sent to Yarmouth. Fishing had become a local activity only.

'The sea giveth, and the sea taketh away', to corrupt an apophthegm. The town's rapid decline during the hundred years or so until the middle of the eighteenth century was hastened by the destructive force of the sea. There was a general rise in sea level. In 1665 Charles Goodwyn's Rental listed 141 tenements of the Lower Town, but 'twenty-two that were, lately, are now overflowed by the sea. No rent is now paid.' Eleven years later, the situation was so critical that the yeoman, William Jeffery, appealed to the justices of the peace of Lewes for assistance in the shape of a pier or some other defence.

It was not given. Jeffery's gloomy prediction that 'the parish of Brighthelmston [was] in danger of being swallowed up by the rageing of the sea' came to pass in the early years of the following century. Daniel Defoe's account of the 'late dreadful tempest in November 27th 1703' records the devastation it brought, and the loss of several vessels and many of their crew. Less than two years later, the Town Book records how 'another dreadful storm reached the town. . . . Every habitation under the cliff was utterly demolished and its very site concealed from the owners' knowledge beneath a mound of shingle.' From 1705 onwards no record exists of a Lower Town in the parish of Brighton.

As the foreshore was gradually swallowed up, so fishing and freight-carrying vessels were less able to beach. By 1687 the town's customs office was closed because of the decline in trade. And as trade declined, so work became scarcer and the population fell. In 1600, the town accommodated maybe four thousand inhabitants; the *Magna Britannia* of 1730 recorded less than half that number. What's more, the remaining populace were gripped by poverty. In 1689 the town's churchwardens complained to the JPs of Lewes that 'the charges of relieving and maynteyning the poore of the said parish is so greate and burdensome to the inhabitants thereof that they are not able to bare the charges thereof.'

Some assistance came from neighbouring parishes, but they promptly fabricated their own poor. In 1708 a general three halfpenny rate was raised throughout eastern Sussex for the relief of poverty in Brighton. In 1727 a new poor-house was built in Market Street. But poverty didn't go away: of 363 houses listed in the Poor Rate Book of 1744, 250 were exempted from paying the rate.

The raging sea didn't go away either. Despite the Church Briefs, which funded the building of two wooden groynes between 1723 and 1724, the *Magna Britannia* urged 'speedy care . . . to stop the encroachments of the sea', lest the town become 'utterly depopulated'. By 1743 there were three more groynes. Defoe questioned the investment of public funds. In his book of 1724, *A Tour through the whole island of Great Britain*, he observed that 'the expense of which [groynes] the brief expressly says will be £8,000 which if one were to look on the town would seem to be more than all the houses in it are worth'.

But the sea, the villain itself, was about to repay that investment – with interest.

CHAPTER FOUR

The Doctor's Prescription

Drink half a pint of sea water every morning at five of the clock, and to avoid the inconvenience of being thirsty which frequently attends it . . . sleep an hour or two afterwards.

Dr Russell's advice to a patient (*c.* 1750)

Is this not Heaven compared to Pall Mall?

G.S. Carey (*The Balnea*, 1799)

I n 1750 a physician from the county town of Lewes effectively invented the seaside. In so doing, the good doctor initiated the transformation, in less than half a century, of a down-at-heel fishing community into an adventure playground for the rich and fashionable.

Despite glimmers of a revival, Brighton was still a fairly wretched place. A declining fishing industry, rising unemployment and the cost of defending the shoreline against the sea were sapping the town's life blood. And then along came Doctor Richard Russell. In 1750 his *Dissertation on the Use of Sea Water in Diseases of the Glands* was published in its Latin original. Repeated pirated English translations soon followed and, in 1752, Russell was honoured as a Fellow of the Royal Society of Medicine. So what was it that created such a big splash?

Russell promoted sea-bathing not as exercise, but as a kind of medicated bath. Moreover, as a preparation for the cold plunge, he prescribed the drinking by the pint of the efficacious, God-given waters of the sea. Yet this, and the associated treatments he advocated – seaweed rubs and hot fermentations and pills made from crabs' eyes, woodlice, adders, snails, cuttlefish bone and other delicacies – weren't really that radical. In effect, he was reactivating Greek medical theories of thalassotherapy: theories still practised today in centres like Biarritz in France. And people had been taking the waters in spa towns for centuries. At Bath, for example, sufferers

Dr Russell: inventor of the seaside?

from flatulence and cold humours could join the maids who longed to eat coal; while patients wishing to strengthen their brain could travel to Tunbridge Wells. Russell now prescribed sea-water for such complaints as consumption, obstructions, abcesses and tumours.

Despite the salutory iodine, the value would have lain not so much in the water itself, but in the regime that went with it. Here Russell was a true pioneer. A disciplined routine of cleanliness, exercise and fresh air would have been alien to those sectors of the urban populace either too poor to escape their dark, dirty hovels or sufficiently wealthy to overindulge their appetites.

But it was some regime! The combination of drinking some salt cordial at five in the morning followed by the shock of being plunged into a cruel sea by some hooded harridan employed as your 'dipper' should surely have finished off the more faint-hearted patient. Yet Russell could claim successes – for washing is always a great notion, lungfulls of ozone help invigorate the body and the sea-water tonic would have purged the most abused of digestive systems.

Hooded harridans dipping their victims

AUGUST. — Bathing at Brighton.

As the inscription on Russell's tombstone reads, 'the ocean washes away the ills of Mankind'.

The man and his ideas were soon the talk of fashionable drawing rooms. Patients started to come to Brighton. By 1753 Russell had moved from Lewes and set up in Russell House, then the largest house in town. Today it is the site of the Royal Albion Hotel; a plaque urges one to seek his monument by looking around at this queen of resorts. Russell's influence was indisputable. Sea-bathing was already common practice in the spa town of Scarborough, but people like the Revd William Clarke of Buxton, who wrote (in 1736) of 'sunning ourselves upon the beach at Brighthelmston' after 'the morning business [of] bathing in the sea', were regarded as freaks by all those who believed that the damp sea atmosphere and salt breezes were detrimental to health.

So how on earth did one man and his dissertation bring about such far-reaching change? In truth, that change might not have been so total, so permanent, had his work not been carried on after his death in 1759 (ironically, on a visit to London). Two disciples were to make up a medical trinity which ensured that the Brighton boom was not just a flash in the pan: Doctors Anthony Relhan and John Awsiter.

Dr Relhan took over a large part of Russell's practice after leaving Dublin under a cloud – for prescribing too many of Doctor Robert James's notorious powders. In his *Short History of Brighton with Remarks on its Air and an Analysis of its Waters*, published in 1761, Relhan emphasized Brighton's natural advantages: the purity of the air, the distance from the 'noxious steams of perspiring trees and every other cause aiding to produce a damp putrid atmosphere'; and the absence of a river and concomitant freedom 'from the insalutary vapour of stagnant water'. He gave his seal of approval to the chalky ground and the various waters – of the sea, the wells and the Chalybeate Spring of St Anne's Well (which Russell had also prescribed to his patients).

What's more, he produced a set of statistics which seemed to support his idea that the longevity of the local populace was due to their 'living in a constant sea vapour' in a place where 'neither dropsical nor chloritic complaints, pleurisies, nor quincies, nor any other inflammatory ones prevail'. As one of the first to analyse birth and death rates, Relhan concluded that the local rate of mortalities was half that of London. Moreover, between June and September 1760, despite 'the very tottering state of health at their arrival', not one of the four hundred visitors to Brighton died.

Add ingredients such as those recorded in *The Stranger in Brighton* of 1824, namely 'its vicinity to the metropolis, . . . the unrestrained rides on the South Downs, and the pleasantness of the situation', a benign 'Spanish' climate, and cheap land and labour resulting from the prolonged economic depression, and the recipe for growth begins to emerge.

In 1768 Dr Awsiter joined Relhan. He was responsible for 'civilizing' the harsh regimen propounded by their celebrated predecessor. Although he still advocated sea-bathing (particularly as a cure for sterility), his pamphlet, *Thoughts on Brighthelmston – Concerning Sea-Bathing and Drinking Sea-Water with some directions for their use* (1768), proposed the mixing of new milk to sea-water for the sake of delicate stomachs and, crucially, the building of sea-water baths to provide *warm* sea-water to open pores and obviate the dangers of fatigue, exposure to rough seas and cold air. The following year, Awsiter's baths were built in Pool Valley: six cold baths, a showering bath and one hot bath supplied with sea-water pumped from the sea by a steam engine. Bathing could now become a year-round activity.

Writing in 1850, Edwin Lee observed that Brighton, at this time, 'had already obtained a certain degree of reputation among the upper classes of society as a watering place'. Of the four hundred or so visitors already noted in 1760, it is likely that the majority were from the gentry

Early visitors probably came in their own carriages

of Sussex and southern England. In 1794 four thousand three hundred visitors were estimated to have stayed in the town; many of them would have been aristocrats and upper middle-class professionals from the metropolis. The figure reflects a steady improvement in communications. Although there was a coaching service from Brighton to London as early as 1732, John Burton was describing roads in 1751 'which were most abominable . . . rather in the nature of cattle trackways'. The first wave of visitors probably came in their own carriages. By 1766, however, Mr J. Tubbs's new 'Flying Machines' were halving the journey time to one day and increased competition was bringing down prices – from a fare of 16s in 1762 to one of 14s in 1770. Nevertheless, arrival times on some timetables were qualified by the proviso 'God permitting', and travel by coach to and from Brighton in the eighteenth century was fraught with such hazards as cold weather, bolting horses and drunken coachmen.

Visitors were also coming from the continent. For the moment, there were no hostilities with the French. Sufficient passengers on both sides of the Channel warranted the opening in 1764 of a packet service between Brighton and Dieppe. Two schooners, the *Princess Caroline* and *The Industry*, made one return journey each per week for a fare of a guinea each way.

Potential patients, however, were not making the journey to Brighton in such numbers simply for the sake of the waters. In 1763 Chief Justice Wilmot wrote that 'of all the public places I have seen, I like none so well as Brighthelmstone'. Though it was becoming a place to see, its success depended on it being the place to be seen. Relhan's prescription of the Chalybeate spring waters for 'bodies labouring under the consequences of irregular living and illicit pleasures' reads as an open invitation to the rich and dissolute. It was the combination of 'silken folly' and 'bloated disease', to use G.S. Carey's memorable phrase, which so transformed Brighton in the latter part of the century.

Like all fashionable spa towns, it needed spa town facilities to satisfy the demand for health and pleasure. Local entrepreneurs were only too willing to provide them. As Dyke Road became the main artery from the north, so the coaches would deposit their visitors at the inns of North Street and Castle Square. During 1766 and 1767 the Old Ship and Castle Inns added two magnificent, rival Assembly Rooms: suitably splendid venues for balls, promenading, cards and public breakfasts. And as Brighton came to rival Bath as *the* social watering place, so it borrowed the other town's Master of Ceremonies to orchestrate the season. The suggestion is that from 1764–70, Captain William Wade mastered ceremonies in Brighton during the summer and Bath during the winter. Then Wade left Bath for good to become Brighton's first full-time MC for the next forty years or so. His sway was akin to that of

Promenading on the 'cheerful
Steine'

a potentate's. All visitors literally paid their respects: a guinea for entry
into a visitors' book. In return, Wade would issue invitations and effect
introductions (a necessary service if you were an impecunious
gentleman, say, on the prowl for unprotected ladies and lone dowagers).

Variety would have been the spice of Captain Wade's itineraries.
The *Brighton & Hove Gazette's Fin de Siècle Review* of 1897
described the 'public concerts, private evening parties, card playing
and tea drinking, boating and bathing, and hunting and riding out'.
And then there was always the promenade. Promenading was not,
initially, a sea front phenomenon. Rather, the pathways of the
'cheerful Steine' represented the dandies' Mecca – until the brief but
dazzling reign of the Promenade Grove Pleasure Gardens. Opened in
1793 on the site of today's Pavilion Gardens, they contained walks,
arbours, a music salon and dancing platform, and offered, until their
closure in 1802, such entertainments as pony racing, lotteries,
concerts, public breakfasts and spectacular firework displays.

When the weather let down the hedonistic 'patients', the
renowned prescription libraries, which opened in the 1760s and '70s,
provided indoor social clubs. Baker's Library and Rotunda,
Woodgate's Library and Bowen's Library, for example, all
strategically situated by the Steine, assumed a reputation for the
'free intermingling of the sexes'. They offered patrons the
opportunity for painting and sketching, music, cards, gambling,

raffles, billiards, gossip and – perish the idea – a little reading. Nor will Brighton ever be complete without the theatre. In 1764 the Chichester Company of Comedians hired a barn on the Steine and presented a double bill of *The Busy Body* and, topically enough, *The Mock Doctor.* From 1774 onwards, North Street provided the first of several sites for a permanent theatre, and soon established what has become a long-standing tradition of first-class productions.

Other pastimes on offer were not so innocent. Most seemed to involve blood or money, or both. Cock-fighting, bear-baiting and badger-baiting were all popular 'sports'. The *Lewes Journal* of 1774 described 'the constant rattle of the dice at the Rattle traps' in the Raffle shops of the Steine, which offered punters quality prizes such as 'muslin, chintz, cambricks and tea': an aristocratic ancestor, it seems, of prize bingo. Large sums of money would change hands at prize fights, even cricket matches! Two packs of hounds were kept for the purpose of hunting and the infamous Duke of Cumberland, the Butcher of Culloden, used to organize special events involving the release of stags on the Steine. Even old-time religion came to have its price: the Chapel Royal was built in 1793 as a business enterprise. The Revd Thomas Hudson was granted parliamentary approval to 'seek profits from the pew rents by obtaining the highest prices that can be gotten for the same'. The Prince of Wales was to pay 13 guineas a year for his pew – until Hudson's sermon on the sin of adultery drove him away!

Though one of its illustrious visitors, Dr Samuel Johnson, complained that 'if one had a mind to hang oneself it would be difficult to find a tree on which to fasten the rope', Brighton's charms were luring literati and aristocrats alike. Cumberland was not the only one of the king's brothers to visit the town: the Dukes of Gloucester and York had already graced Brighton with their presence. In 1771 the Duke of Marlborough bought a house on the Steine. By 1777 the poet G.S. Carey was describing the town as a place 'becramm'd with quality'.

Such an influx of visitors was bound to have a dramatic impact on this erstwhile fishing community. For the next century or so, the local economy was to be based on the upper classes, and their twin pursuits of health and pleasure. As early as 1761 J.G. Bishop was describing how 'lodging houses were . . . regarded by the townsfolk as a new El Dorado'.

There was money to be made on the beaches, too. A rare breed of professional, the 'dipper' ('those hideous amphibious animals', as the artist Constable was to dub them), would help tentative clients down the steps of their bathing machine, a kind of beach hut on wheels, before immersing them in the sea. Such was the renown of Martha Gunn, the queen of the dippers, that she was commemorated as a Toby

Martha Gunn's grave in St Nicholas's churchyard

Brighton 1779: a growing population, but a self-contained town

Jug and in a music hall song (as a 'kind of female Neptune'). Sixty glorious years of dipping clients – presumably without calamity – no doubt contributed to her longevity. She died in 1815 at the age of eighty-eight, but not before she – and Smoaker John Miles, the king of the profession – had enjoyed the friendship of the Prince of Wales.

More jobs meant more people and, by 1783, the population had risen once more – to three thousand five hundred. However, it was not all wealth and pleasure by the sea. The indigenous underclass was swollen by an ever-increasing retinue of servants and retainers. Local society polarized into two distinct sectors: the 'haves' and the 'have-nots' who serviced them. Far from being eradicated, poverty was to remain a constant fact of Brighton life.

From 1773 for the next eighty years or so, the burgeoning town was to be governed by a body of commissioners. The sixty-four men of

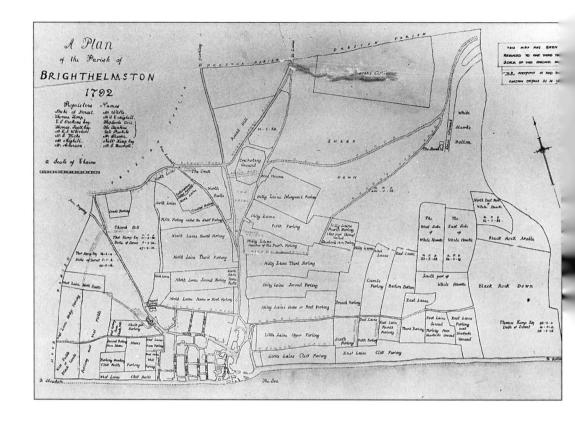

substance, appointed town commissioners under the Brighton Town Act, were granted substantial powers. While the parish vestry still maintained responsibility for the poor, the commissioners replaced the old Society of Twelve, and assumed responsibility for paving, lighting, elementary building regulations, maintenance of pure water, removal of nuisances and cleaning of the streets. They could require inhabitants to sweep in front of their houses between the hours of 8 a.m. and 10 a.m. every day except Sunday. Moreover, they were empowered to levy a local rate of up to 3*s* in the pound for general upkeep of the town and to borrow up to £3,000 for the building of a new Market House.

Such a sum was secured partly against a new tax on all coal landed on the beaches. As *The Stranger in Brighton* records, this tax of 6*d* per 'chaldron' would provide sufficient funds for 'building and repairing groynes, in order to render the coast more safe and commodious for vessels'. The duty was increased in 1810 to 3*s* a chaldron and by the 1840s the coal tax was bringing in a revenue of between £6–8,000 each year. It became essential to re-establish a Customs at Brighton, particularly since the latter part of the eighteenth century represented a kind of golden age of smuggling. Despite such

The open field system: the origins of . . .

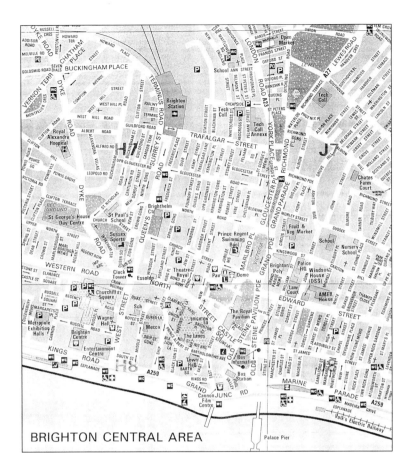

BRIGHTON CENTRAL AREA

. . . Brighton's distinctive street pattern

seizures as 1,680 lb of tobacco and thirty-nine casks of Geneva (in 1789), it is estimated that between 1776 and 1783 the smugglers accounted for about 25 per cent of the total value of trade. Of Brighton's numerous legends, it is thought that some are attributable to smugglers. According to the most famous, the Lady Edona died of grief in St Nicholas's churchyard. Scanning the horizon for the ship which was bringing her betrothed back from Byzantium, she watched it strike some rocks and sink with the loss of all hands. The fable of the returning ghost ship (at midnight each year, on 17 May) would have helped to keep people indoors on dark nights – when smugglers were afoot!

This is romantic stuff. But smuggling was a crime and there was nothing romantic about other crimes recorded during the era. The body of a murdered prostitute was found by men cleaning a well and a certain Anne Boon threw her dead child into a pigsty in the hope that it would be eaten. Apart from smuggling and murder, assault, robbery and absconding (abandoning one's family to the care of the parish) were the other principal categories of crime.

Most recorded crimes were motivated by poverty. For all the amenities, conditions were still squalid for most of the locals. Although the town was growing to accommodate an expanding population, until about 1780 almost all the urban development took place within an increasingly crowded Old Town – and much of that was in the form of poor-quality housing for workers.

Nevertheless, 'quality' was beginning to leave its mark. West Street was considered to be the most exclusive part of town in the 1770s, and Ship Street became the centre (as, indeed, it is today) for lawyers, solicitors and other 'professionals'. Several large houses were built along the western edge of the Steine, which was partly enclosed with wooden railings in 1776 – much to the fishermen's understandable anger. It was the Steine's most illustrious resident, the Duke of Marlborough, in conjunction with the Prince of Wales, who helped to dry out the promenade by diverting the occasional Wellesbourne into a sewer.

Demand for housing could not long go unsatisfied. Between 1770 and 1800 the number of houses in Brighton doubled. Slowly the town began to spread east, west and northwards, as the developers bought up land from the proprietors of the five open fields or 'tenantry laines' which enclosed the town. The land was sub-divided into furlongs, which were separated from each other by narrow 'leakways' and further sub-divided into paulpieces. That the builders found it convenient to buy and develop the land piecemeal, a furlong at a time, accounts largely for the modern town's distinctive street pattern. Though the Little Laine, east of the Steine, was the first to be systematically developed in the late eighteenth century, the old field system is best illustrated by a study of the North Laine's topography. Compare the map of 1792 with the detail from the modern street map. Church Street, North Road, Gloucester Street and Trafalgar Street would all have been leakways, while the small parallel streets of terraced housing, which link the main thoroughfares, would have been paulpieces.

From the 1780s onwards, Brighton grew in a series of prodigious leaps and bounds. A poem of 1825 describes how 'Speculation plants its hod/On every foot of freehold sod/From Rottingdean to Worthing'. If any one individual was responsible for such a boom, it was George Prince of Wales. In 1783, at the age of twenty-one, he first came to Brighton to try the sea-cure. He approved of the cure and the place, thereby sealing the success of both. The world of high fashion followed apace. As G.S. Carey observed in 1799, 'the eagles and hawks for ever gather round the highest rocks'.

CHAPTER FIVE

Jewels in the Crown

I join with the great Michael Angelo in thanking George IV for inventing Brighton.

from *Brighton: the Road, the Place, the People* (1862)

I marvel not that friends tell friends
And every day Brighton extends
Its circuses and crescents

from 'Ode to Mahomed' (1822)

George IV: Brighton's patron saint – or sinner?

In his introduction to *Victorian and Edwardian Brighton from Old Photographs*, Sir John Betjeman wrote of vendors in the Lanes denouncing George IV as 'a drunken profligate, a liar and as false as the stucco which covered the buildings associated with him'. Particularly as a prince of the realm, there is little doubt that George was a womanizer and bon viveur who did most things to excess: he was quite capable of paying 90 guineas each (in 1805!) for a pair of Brussels lace handkerchiefs. But 'Prinny', as he was affectionately known, was also artistic, intelligent, witty, charming and generous to a fault. There is little doubt that Brighton owes its pre-eminence to the man dubbed its 'patron saint' (or sinner!).

It is hardly surprising then, that his first visit to the town, in September 1783, should be marked by fireworks and a salute fired from the battery (which, tragically, killed the gunner). Quite apart from his impact on Brighton's fashionable reputation, his influence was soon apparent. The Prince of Wales was a great champion of the Whig party, and what with his presence and that of his friend, Charles James Fox, the party's flamboyant leader, Brighton soon became a Mecca for liberals. Of the new housing developments which reflected the rapid increase of visitors, those adjoining the Steine on North Parade were painted with the Whig colours; the two survivors are known to this day as 'the Blue and Buff'.

Prinny's early patronage of the recently established Brighton races guaranteed its place on the social calendar. A keen horseman himself, as a young man he rode, reputedly, from Brighton to London and back again in ten hours. Fifty miles or so away from the strict paternal gaze of the king, Brighton was also just close enough to allow him to return promptly to the capital in an emergency. Perfect! From his second visit (in 1784) on, the Prince of Wales was to visit his seaside playground as frequently as possible.

His love affair with the town was soon cemented by one of his many affairs of the heart. George, the lover, preferred the company of older women: his first, at the age of fifteen, was his mother's twenty-three-year-old lady in waiting. Following a multitude of amorous indiscretions, the Prince of Wales then met Maria Fitzherbert in 1784. His wooing of this striking, wealthy woman – a widow twice over – knew no bounds. Being a Catholic and knowing that marriage was out of the question, Mrs Fitzherbert never encouraged him, and frequent tears and tantrums resulted – even a feigned suicide attempt.

Mrs Fitzherbert: the striking widow

Eventually, after a self-enforced exile in France, she capitulated. In December 1785 the couple were married secretly – by a bribed cleric. They returned to separate houses in Brighton, where they became the town's social monarchs. Thanks to his 'clerk of the kitchen', Louis Weltje, the Prince of Wales rented Thomas Kemp's 'farmhouse', with its romantic prospect across the pastoral promenade of the Steine. But though his time there was reputedly the happiest time of his life, the good life of sober fidelity could not and did not last.

Weltje was no ordinary clerk. Chef, confidant, friend and general factotum, Weltje was also a very rich man who was able to negotiate the funds (or some of them) to satisfy his employer's insatiable appetite to spend, spend, spend. Soon, the farmhouse required alterations to befit an heir to the throne. While Weltje acquired the lease on the property, the Prince of Wales rented it from him (for £1,000 per year!) and engaged Henry Holland to carry out the conversion. One hundred and fifty workmen were set to work and, despite several deaths on the construction site, the building was ready for occupation in three months. Though it was described by one critic as looking like a madhouse, the Marine Pavilion, as it was known, was a modest, two-storey classical villa in the shape of a letter 'E', with a central domed saloon braced by six Ionic columns. The wings either side featured the bow fronts and iron balconies which were to be hallmarks of so many of Brighton's houses built during the next fifty years.

The brilliant French-style interior decor was more in keeping with the period of wild living which began with the prince's occupation of his new home on 6 July 1787. Here was a much more suitable venue for entertaining his cronies. Gamblers, drunkards, horsemen,

A madhouse? Henry Holland's
Marine Pavilion

wits, writers, aristocrats and plutocrats, all and sundry were accepted
into his circle – provided, that is, that they weren't boring. Fox, the
playwright Sheridan, the Duke of Queensbery, who bathed daily in
milk, Honest George Hangar, who was once ridden by a jockey
across the Steine in a race against a fat bullock, Lady Letitia Lade,
an ex-mistress famous for her swearing, the barking-mad Barrymore
quartet: many were Irish, many were Whigs, and most of them were
dissolute, irresponsible and pretty wild. 'Morning rides, dissipation,
noise and nonsense' was, according to the *Morning Post*, 'a
complete account of all that passes at Brighthelmston'. When
Hangar complained that the Pavilion's patent stoves were making
him as 'hot as hell', Sheridan informed him that they were being
'prepared in this world for our lot in the next'.

Such entertainment was not to Mrs Fitzherbert's liking. For the sake
of propriety, and probably for her own sanity, she lived separately. At
the centre of such constantly high society, it is not surprising that her
husband did not remain faithful for long. She was remarkably tolerant
of his infidelities until Lady Francis Jersey, a beautiful grandmother of
forty, proved the final straw that broke the couple up.

The prince's life-style was definitely not to the liking of his father. By now, his debts amounted to something like £600,000. Father and son struck an uneasy deal. To quote some doggerel of 1794: 'There's Caroline of Brunswick, will give her pretty hand/If you'll but pay my debts sir, I'll take her at command'. Caroline was Protestant, but 'pretty' she wasn't – a fact that Cruikshank and other contemporary cartoonists so ruthlessly exploited. Though the couple married in 1795, the Prince of Wales hated the sight of her and in his will of the following year, he bequeathed 'everything to . . . the wife of my heart and soul' and 'to *her* that is called the Princess of Wales . . . one shilling'. A second frantic wooing of Mrs Fitzherbert culminated in a public reconciliation in 1800. For her part, Caroline bore her rival no animosity; however, her subsequent scandalous life was an appropriate riposte to her husband.

Maria Fitzherbert's forgiveness was dependent on the Pope's blessing and his proviso that the prince 'is penitent and amends his ways'. The next few years may have been happy ones for the couple, but they were marked by a further frenzy of financial activity. In 1802, perhaps prompted by a gift of some Chinese wallpaper, the Prince of Wales commissioned the Crace firm to redecorate the

The Dome: luxury accommodation for lucky horses

Pavilion in chinoiserie. By 1808 he had commissioned William Porden to build Steine House (today's YMCA) for Mrs Fitzherbert; he had closed the Promenade Grove Gardens, bought the land and diverted the north-bound traffic which had once passed by his Pavilion to the New Road; he had bought the Pavilion outright from Weltje's trustees; and Porden had finally finished his outlandish stables and riding school. Built on the lawns of the Marine Pavilion and inspired by Indian architecture, together they cost around £55,000 to build. The remarkable Dome (as it became known) housed the prince's horses in forty-four separate stables and prompted sneers that his horses were better accommodated than the prince himself.

So how did he afford such expenditure? The answer is, he couldn't – which is one reason why the stables and the riding school took so long to complete, and one reason why the grandiloquent plans of Porden and Repton to match the Pavilion to its new outhouses were shelved. The Prince of Wales simply exercised his power and station to run up prodigious debts. Edward Saunders, for example, who undertook the timber work for the stables, died a broken man in 1805: destitute through non-payment of around £11,000. The story goes that Thomas Attree, the town's leading solicitor, was presented with a drawing of the Prince of Wales in lieu of some (considerable) conveyancing fees.

Remember, too, that this orgy of expenditure took place in the context of the Napoleonic Wars. Little wonder, then, that the profligate prince should be the target for cartoonists, journalists and politicians alike – particularly once Prinny had assumed the mantle of Prince Regent in 1811, following his father's final bout of madness. Here, perhaps, the counsel for the defence should remind detractors that the ever-degenerating, ever-swelling 'Prince of Whales' had once been a lively, highly intelligent, artistically gifted child subjected to a stifling regime of solitary study and floggings. Even frustrated, now, in his yearning to go to war, this life of excess may have stemmed from a creative will too long suppressed.

So, once more Brighton was witness to a war against the old cross-Channel adversary. If anything, a military presence in the town provided 'silken folly' with yet more temptations. With Belle Vue field transformed into a military camp, the cavalry barracked on the road to Lewes and the infantry at the bottom of Church Street, it is not surprising that Lydia Bennett should describe Brighton as 'the place to get husbands' in Jane Austen's *Pride and Prejudice*. In such a place 'where the temptations must be greater than at home', Wickham, the husband Lydia 'got', managed to run up gambling debts of 'more than a thousand pounds'. Gambling had become almost a fever, with men prepared to gamble, it was said, on two flies on a wall. With card games, cricket, boxing, horse-racing, running and walking races on the Steine, cock-fighting and dog-fighting, there was ample opportunity to win and lose large sums of money.

Thackeray, whose epic novel *Vanity Fair* is set partly against the backdrop of a military Brighton, described the town as always looking 'brisk, gay and gaudy, like a harlequin's jacket'. While the common militia underwent the kinds of conditions which provoked a revolt in 1794, for the gentility, those heady early years of the new century provided a wealth of diversions. Though William Forth never quite enjoyed the influence or repute of his predecessor as Master of Ceremonies, the social attractions pulled the crowds in as never before. The lists of visitors read like pages from *Debrett*. There were balls and carriage rides and promenades. There were mock sea battles and chaotic military manoeuvres on the Downs to observe. There were elegant women and ostentatious dandies to gawk at. From 1807, there were celebrated thespians to admire at the new Theatre Royal in New Road (where its first patron, the Prince of Wales, rented a box for £25 per year). There were more libraries, more bathing machines and more public baths. And Thackeray's heroine, Becky Sharp, was not the only one to bring a telescope 'to bear upon the bathing-machines on the beach' and enjoy an early form of the peep-show.

The 'Shampooing Surgeon' – Sake Dene Mahomed

And there was shampooing. Born in Patna, India, Sake Dene Mahomed had opened his Indian Vapour Baths on the site of the Queen's Hotel. Though fame and fortune didn't arrive overnight, he was later to be appointed shampooing surgeon to George IV. His pseudo-medical treatise on shampooing of 1822 ran to three editions, and he reinforced his claim that he could cure asthma, paralysis, rheumatism, sciatica, lumbago, contractions and much more by turning his establishment into a kind of Lourdes shrine with (supposedly) discarded crutches, leg irons, spine stretchers and club-foot reformers. So how did it work? His patients would be steamed gently under a kind of flannel tent and, once they were 'perspiring freely', Sake Dene would slip his arms through a pair of inlets and knead the patient with 'medicated oils' – a form of aromatherapy massage, in other words. Whether or not 'fat dowagers and wrinkled maids re-bloom[ed] in adolescence', as the 'Ode to Mahomed' claimed, Sake Dene's alleged age of 102 years testified to the benefits of shampooing.

For the lucky ones, then, they were golden years. But if the Regency is synonymous with elegance and excess, it is equally known for its remarkable architecture. And nothing set the seal on the era like the final flowering of the prince's Pavilion. In 1815 the Napoleonic Wars came to an end; after twenty-three years of conflict, Britain was financially exhausted. Nevertheless, the

The Music Room: probably the finest room in the world

effective monarch was determined to easternize his Brighton palace. His relationship with Mrs Fitzherbert was now extinguished, and with no one except his ministers, the media and the general public to admonish him, the Prince Regent commissioned the great John Nash to design and build him an oriental palace.

The cost mounted daily, and though his prime minister told him that 'Parliament will not vote one shilling for defraying such expenses', the prince was not to be deflected. The immense crystal gasolier in the Banqueting Room cost £5,613 alone! In January 1820 the prince was crowned King George IV, and by the following year the new Royal Pavilion was virtually complete. The resulting Gothic Indo-Chinese fantasy had many critics: it was called an 'enlarged China-shop', and a combined 'Turkish Harem, and a Russian Cremlin'. Memorably, the Revd Sydney Smith described how 'one would have thought the Dome of St Paul's Cathedral had come to Brighton and pupped'.

The interior was completed in 1823 and the king apparently confessed that he cried for joy on contemplating the splendours. The exterior is remarkable, but the interior is truly extraordinary. The author of *A Day or Two at Brighton* (1852) wrote of the 'bronzed serpents at your feet, and horrible dragons overhead; boa constrictors twist themselves round the pillars, and birds of prey soar among the lights'. It was 'comparable to nothing which has been reared in this country either before or since'. Certainly the combined contributions of Nash, George himself and the interior designers, Frederick Crace and Robert Jones, are unique. But, aesthetics aside, the unprecedented use of cast iron, the wall-to-wall carpeting, the gas fittings and prototype central-heating system made it a technological showpiece.

BRIGHTON, ENGLAND'S FAVOURITE WATERING PLACE—1825.

Carriages, promenaders and the Chain Pier

Whatever the cost and whatever the criticisms, the king now had a seaside palace fit for a royal aesthete, and Brighton was to reap the rewards of his extravagance. Today around three hundred and forty thousand visitors a year come to marvel at the Music Room, say, or the Great Kitchen where the king's celebrated chef, Carême, once conjured up a banquet with 112 dishes for George and his guests. Then, too, the Pavilion brought still more visitors to Brighton.

More visitors meant more amenities. The sea front was opened up to carriages and promenaders with the opening of King's Road in January 1821. More promenaders were diverted from the Steine when Captain Samuel Brown's Chain Pier opened in November 1823 in response to the rise in cross-channel traffic following the end of the war. With it, in fact (and despite unfulfilled plans to build a harbour), Brighton became, for a time, Britain's busiest cross-channel port. That same year, Lamprell's Baths, a great dome construction known as 'The Bunion', opened on the sea front, and James Ireland laid out the Royal Pleasure Gardens just north of the Level. In June 1825 Dr F. A. Struve opened his German Spa at the south-western corner of today's Queen's Park. Its pump room and bottled mineral water, concocted to imitate celebrated German spa waters, proved so successful that the spa was later said to be the reason for sending '*real* patients' to Brighton. In 1826 the Royal Albion Hotel was built on the site of Dr Russell's house; like its older sister, the Royal York, it faced a Steine now declining in importance. In 1829 the elegant, luxurious and sea-facing Bedford Hotel opened its doors. The incredible building boom of the 1820s also gave rise to some of the town's finest churches; Charles Barry's St Peter's was to provide the swelling town with a more substantial parish church. By the end of the decade the Grand Junction Road was opened, linking King's Road to the west and the embryonic Marine Parade to the east, thus providing a through road along the whole of Brighton's ever-elongating sea front.

And more amenities meant still more visitors. These years witnessed a golden age of coaching: improved roads, lighter coaches and fierce competition brought the journey time down to around six hours (though at some cost to human and equine life). By 1835 thirty-six coaches were running daily between London and Brighton (and around half that number from other towns), carrying a hundred and seventeen thousand passengers in that one year for a fare of around 21*s* (inside) or 12*s* (outside).

There was a crying need to accommodate people. Despite the town being dubbed 'one big lodging-house', and despite the grand hotels which sprang up in the 1820s, there were now thousands of visitors during the high season who needed a roof over their heads.

J.B. Otto's Royal Crescent

'Ammonite fossils' and other characteristics of the Regency style (Oriental Place)

There were those of the ilk of the Duke of Devonshire, the Marquis of Bristol and the former prime minister, George Canning, who settled in the town. And there were those disparaged by a writer of 1810 as 'moneyed men [who] can pass for men of worth'. Builders and speculators were not slow to spot a niche in the market.

In the year of the king's first visit, 1783, the town's population was approximately 3,500. By 1801 the first census showed it had doubled to 7,339. Between 1811 and 1821 it doubled again from 12,012 to 24,429. Even before the building boom of the 1820s, Brighton was slowly but inevitably expanding geographically: as far, by 1820, as Regency Square to the west, Richmond Terrace to the north of the Steine and Royal Crescent to the east, where the fourteen elegant lodging houses 'for the better accommodation of fashionable visitors', conceived by the West Indian merchant and speculator, J.B. Otto, represented the first out-of-town development. Completed in 1807, these houses, faced with black glazed 'mathematical tiles', proved a more permanent tribute to Brighton's royal patron than the plaster statue, which lost an arm and its nose before it disappeared in 1819. The prince was not amused.

Development was dictated largely by the fashionable romantic interest in the sea. The cliff top was the favoured site for the most superior dwellings. The rows of parallel streets, built at right angles from the front for the slightly inferior resident, often display the characteristic Regency bow windows and iron balconies which allowed a glimpse of the waves.

Many of the finest examples of the Regency style were built during the boom of the 1820s – after the political Regency period had ended. Unlike Bath, there was no local stone to quarry; a compound of bricks and pebble known as 'bungaroush' was often used as a base, and then rendered with stucco to look like stone. The number of houses doubled during this remarkable decade and it is estimated that five million bricks were used in Brighton during 1823 alone.

Many of these monuments to the age bear the hallmarks – the ironwork and the hooded balconies, the ornamental pediments and pilasters with capitals characterized by a motif known as the 'ammonite fossil' (pun intended?) – of a style whose finest exponents were a trio of local architects: Charles Augustus Busby; his partner, Amon Wilds; and his partner's son, Amon Henry Wilds. Their achievements were too many to list, suffice to highlight their crowning glories: the self-contained (and immediately successful) Brunswick estate to the west, designed with its own market and service streets for the Revd Thomas Scutt (and managed from 1830 by its own commissioners); and Kemp Town to the east.

Herein lies a cautionary tale of speculation. The same Thomas Read Kemp, whose farmhouse accommodated a young Prince of Wales, was

The palatial mansions of Lewes Crescent

a man almost as remarkable as his king. Having inherited land, power, a parliamentary seat and immense wealth from his father, he proceeded to give away much of the land and squander his fortune in a style befitting the monarch. Kemp's town, the Wilds and Busby partnership's first commission, was conceived as an exclusive private estate outside the town's eastern boundary. Work began in 1823, but Kemp's financial situation was soon desperate; five years later, all building work was halted. Though many of the facades were erected, only thirty-six houses were completed – and they sold slowly, probably because of the estate's isolation. Described by the *Brighton Gazette* as 'an outlaw from his own country', the ruined Kemp died in Paris in 1844, several years before his estate was properly finished. The palatial mansions of Sussex Square and Lewes Crescent, flanked by Chichester Terrace to the west and Arundel Terrace to the east, may represent less than half of the original conception, but Kemp Town offers some of the finest examples of Regency architecture in Britain. 'Like Belgravia,' wrote the author of *A Day or Two at Brighton* in 1852, 'they stand in almost voiceless and dignified seclusion.'

Not everyone was so enamoured of Brighton's new face. Turner and Constable came to paint here, but the latter described the town, in 1827, as the 'off-scouring of London' and found 'nothing here for a painter but the sea and the sky' (although one might add the Chain Pier). This edifice was resented by the boatmen, who once earned a good wage ferrying bilious cross-Channel passengers to and from boats 'half swamped among the breakers'. And there were vehement protests by

The acceptable face of Regency Brighton

the ever-dwindling corps of fishermen when the Steine was enclosed in 1823, and the last capstan on the front was removed in 1827.

To turn over the glistening gold Regency coin was to find an image of poverty and squalor. For all the visitors and all the building, employment was mainly seasonal, and any houses built for the lower orders were little more than hovels. The North Laine area was developing as the resort's major service area and an industrial base, but areas like Durham and Petty France were already degenerating into slums as bad as anywhere in Britain. Moreover, the cost of living was higher than in London. Drunkenness, disease, begging and prostitution were rife, and there are references to the practices of wife-selling (at Brighton market) and body-snatching (from St Nicholas's churchyard). Such incidents as the first Brighton trunk murder in 1831 underlined how necessary were the 'watchmen' created as an early police force by the town commissioners.

By 1830 there were an estimated eighteen thousand poor in Brighton. Very often, their only recourse was to seek refuge in the workhouse. One of its most celebrated intermittent residents was Phoebe Hessel, who once fought with distinction (supposedly) in the British army, disguised as a man. She died in 1821 at the age of 108, but not before she had been granted, in 1808, a pension of 10s 6d a week by the Prince of Wales. He had already proved that charity begins in the palace by financing the brief stay of a party of thirty-seven refugee nuns from revolutionary France in October 1792. There was a crying need for charity during this age. A wealth of benevolent and charitable institutions sprang up, sometimes with royal support and generally associated with wealthy patrons and/or the church. There were coal clubs and soup kitchens, self-help, blanket lending, Bible reading and temperance societies. The longest lasting must be the Sussex County Hospital and General Sea Bathing Infirmary, a medical charity founded partly on the Earl of Egremont's money, Kemp's land and Charles Barry's design for a building which still forms the core of today's hospital. Opened in 1828, its patients had to be sponsored by a subscriber willing to guarantee removal and burial expenses. Conditions were fairly insanitary, neither children nor pregnant women were admitted, and entry in the Black Book for such misdemeanours as 'kissing a scrubber' meant discharge with no readmittance.

Under the Town Act of 1810, responsibility for such matters was transferred to thirty 'Directors and Guardians of the Poor'. The number of commissioners was increased to 100, and with the coal tax raised to 3s a chaldron, there was sufficient borrowing power to finance a new Market House (1828–30), and, opposite it in Bartholomews, the grandiose classical town hall (1830–2), which serves the council to this day. The number of commissioners was further increased to 116 under the Town Act of 1825. There was much to occupy these municipal overlords: from the appointment of rubbish 'scavengers', firemen and watchmen to the relocation of slaughter houses and widening of roads.

Though the commissioners were now elected, it was only the major property owners who were eligible to vote. Similarly, the ordinary person was disenfranchised from national affairs. Following the 1832 Reform Act, Brighton was granted two MPs – but only 1,649 of a population of around 41,000 were able to vote for them in the elections of that year. Organizations like the Brighton Political Union had campaigned long and hard for such basic rights as universal suffrage and a secret ballot; a sense of betrayal and disillusionment fuelled an upsurge of radical activity in Brighton throughout the decade. Previously it had found a more temperate voice in the philanthropist, Dr William King, whose journal, *The Cooperator*, broadcast many of the principles of cooperation later espoused by the so-called Rochdale Pioneers. By the end of the decade he had helped to found a mechanics institute and open two co-operative stores. Moreover, following the 1832 débâcle, over five hundred local workers joined trades unions, according to the *Brighton Herald*. And protest found its loudest voice in the mouthpiece of the Radical Registration and Patriotic Association (RRPA), *The Brighton Patriot*. In 1838 the RRPA became the National Charter Association of Brighton; the town, the favourite resort of the nobility, was to become the leading focus in the south for the revolutionary and ultimately ill-fated Chartist crusade.

While his seaside subjects were revolting, the town's 'patron sinner' had grown more conservative in his old age. Disenchanted with the prying crowds, George IV stayed in his Pavilion only three more times after its completion. Following his last visit in 1827, he preferred to hide his bloated body and nurse his gout in Windsor Castle, another of his great creations. Here, the man the Duke of Wellington called 'the first gentleman of Europe' died on 26 June 1830 – still professing his everlasting love for Maria Fitzherbert. Seven years later, she herself died.

Brighton had lost its king and unofficial queen. Despite the patronage of William IV and Queen Adelaide, the town fell into a brief state of depression. Competition from other resorts, unemployment, poverty, poor housing and general economic recession capped the population explosion. There were gloomy forecasts that Brighton's star was burning out. But the depression was short lived. An era of yet more remarkable growth was steaming down the tracks. . . .

CHAPTER SIX

All Change!

To the people of London, the railroad offers the greatest advantages. They can leave their dark, smoky, dirty and unhealthy habitations, and in a couple of hours at the most be inhaling the purest air in the world. . .

Brighton Herald (25 September 1841)

Our first-rate streets are not surpassed, if equalled, in cleanliness and general appearance by any in the world. The streets and districts of the poor, both in filth and general untidiness, and the squalor of the inhabitants, are a disgrace to any civilized people.

Dr William Kebbell (1848)

'N o event', reported the *Brighton Herald*, 'since Brighton has assumed the rank of one of the principal towns in the south of England, has caused so much interest as the opening of the railroad throughout to London.' The day was 23 September 1841. It was a beautiful day; the flags were out and the bells were ringing. 'Every road leading to the terminus was thronged by well-dressed pedestrians and vehicles of every description.' Thousands waited expectantly for the first London to Brighton train. At around 12.20 p.m. anticipation burst forth in a cry of 'Here they come!' 'The first indication was the cloud of steam that poured forth from the mouth of the Patcham Tunnel and the next moment a long dark object was seen swiftly gliding along the line and rapidly increasing in size . . . till . . . the first train from the metropolis came thundering along.' That evening, the town was lit up by the customary firework display.

The railway had well and truly arrived in Brighton. It had been a long time coming. The opening of a branch line to Shoreham the year before was a carrot to win the support of Brighton's neighbouring port for John Rennie's direct route – and end a decade or so of wrangling since a rail link was first proposed in 1823. It took a Parliamentary report to sort out matters and approve Rennie's route in favour of the alternatives. And it took a further year for work to begin, following the passing of the London and Brighton Railway Act in July 1837. With its 5 tunnels, 99 bridges and the 37 arches of

'Here they come!' A train steams towards the new terminus. St Peter's church is to the left

David Mocatta's magnificent viaduct over the Ouse valley, the 50 mile stretch of line took some 6,206 men and 960 horses over three years to complete, at a cost of £2,569,359. Some feat of engineering!

'What effect the railroad will ultimately have upon Brighton', wondered the *Herald* journalist, 'is yet too soon to form an opinion.' It would change the town irrevocably. During the remaining decades of the century, a new epoch of communications effectively brought about a full-scale social revolution.

As a child I was fascinated by that strange hiatus in pioneer TV programming: the interlude. London to Brighton by train in a minute beat the potter's wheel every time. Down through Clapham Junction the steam train would hurtle; then, over the viaduct, before being swallowed whole by the crenellated portals of the Clayton tunnel and coming to rest, mere seconds later, inside the town's Victorian terminus. In reality, the journey took a little longer: around two hours at first. But, compared to previous alternatives, it might as well have been a minute. The railway spelt the end of the coaching industry. Coaching fares plunged to as low as 6s, but it was too late. Despite a subsequent revival prompted by wealthy enthusiasts, the coaches were taken off the road, the horses sold, roadside inns and hotels closed, and the turnpike trusts faced bankruptcy. By 1845 not a single coach was making the journey to London. Ironically, though, the opening of a horse-drawn service from Brighton station to Kemp Town was to revitalize the estate's fortunes and prompt its completion.

That certain of the original scheduled trains on the route were reserved for first-class passengers reflected the London and Brighton South Coast Railway's misguided conception of 'LBSCR traffic [as] a superior class of traffic'. The dream of Brighton as the linchpin of a 'Grand Route' from London to Paris died with Brighton's decline as a channel port – brought about by the opening of a branch line to Newhaven in 1847. LBSCR stock soon fell from £50 to £35 a share.

It was only when the company's second largest shareholder, Rowland Hill (pioneer of the penny post and resident of Hanover Crescent, Brighton), replaced John Harman as chairman of the line in 1844 that the company prospered. Policy now emphasized speed and numbers. Express trains cut the journey time to around an hour and a half, and the first excursion train travelled south on Easter Monday 1844. With third-class Sunday excursion fares cut to 5s return by the following year, demand necessitated trains of up to four engines and fifty-seven carriages to convey the thousand plus travellers per journey. Season tickets were also introduced, and by the time Hill retired the *Railway Chronicle* was calling it the 'best managed line in the kingdom'.

According to the 1897 *Fin de Siècle Review*, 'with the opening up of railway communication, Brighton of-today leaped at one bound with popular favour with the general public'. If it did, the town's character didn't change overnight. Of course, the aspect of the town altered, what with Mocatta's railway terminus (built on a huge man-made plateau cut into the west slope of the London Road combe) and the splendid, curving 400 yd long London Road viaduct (completed in 1846). But though the upper classes now spurned Ramsgate and Margate once the railway opened up these resorts to the masses, this didn't happen in Brighton.

In fact, the ranks of upper-class visitors to Brighton were swollen by refugees from the Kent coast. Rank, fashion and nobility continued to choose Brighton for many years to come. Indeed, royal patronage continued during the reign of William IV. A nautical man, William would walk the Chain Pier every morning during his regular visits to the Pavilion. Faithfully, he ensured the upkeep of his brother's monument, even adding the North Lodge and Gate in 1832. He and his queen, Adelaide, entertained at the Pavilion, and Maria Fitzherbert was a regular guest. Her former husband would have found the new regime as dull as ditch-water. Nevertheless, William and Adelaide were great favourites of the town, and it was only with the coming of Queen Victoria that the love affair between monarchy and resort ended. Her first visit, in October 1837, was marked by a great floral arch, with the word 'Welcome' spelt out in dahlias. But she was to make only four more visits. Unamused by the attentions of a clamouring public, she found the town 'quite a prison'. When the royal train steamed out of Brighton in February 1845, Victoria finally renounced the Pavilion in favour of Osborne House on the Isle of Wight.

Unfortunately, she authorized the systematic stripping of the Pavilion's treasures in preparation for its sale to raise money for the refurbishment of Buckingham Palace. Fixtures and fittings were ripped out, and the booty transported to the capital. As the *New Monthly Magazine* reported in 1851, 'If a pack of Cossacks from the Don . . . had been turned loose into the Pavilion to do their worst, they could not have effected a tithe of the ravages effected by the "Woods & Forests".'

Fortunately, local indignation ran high: a deputation was sent to the Commissioners of Woods and Forests, and a petition of protest was signed by 7,406 inhabitants. As a result, the Pavilion was offered to the town for £53,000. *Punch* sneered that only a tea merchant would want to buy the place. But thanks primarily to Lewis Slight, Clerk to the Brighton Town Commissioners, the protracted and sometimes heated negotiations culminated in a local poll, which approved the purchase – though by the narrowest of margins. Thus it came to pass that, in 1850, the town acquired a priceless treasure for a mere snip. After purchase, the town's new commodity was opened for view at a charge of 6*d* per visitor, and put to work in a variety of ways: by the Brighton Chess Club; as a municipal art gallery; even as a prototype conference centre. The clock tower, erected at the foot of Queen's Road to celebrate Victoria's diamond jubilee in 1887, might appear an offer of thanks from the townspeople to their unwitting benefactress.

The acquisition of the Pavilion might also be symbolized as a mark of transition – from Brighton, playground of privilege to Brighton, Mecca of the masses. But it is premature. Despite the number of excursion trains, the aristocracy was not scared away. What happened was that the fashionable season gradually shifted towards the winter months. 'The "swells"', according to a satire of 1862, 'seldom arrive before November, and generally remain until Christmas.' The 'not so select' visitor now headed to the coast in the summer, while the autumn months tended to cater for the middle classes. In fact, Antony Dale, a founder of the Regency Society (see Chapter Eight), contends, in one of his many books on Brighton, that the thirty years or so following the death of George IV represent the zenith of Brighton's fashionability.

And though the railways offered builders a wider range of raw materials, the Regency style lived on – into the 1860s. Amon Wilds died in 1833; his ex-partner, Charles Busby, died the following year. But his son, Amon Henry Wilds, continued to flourish. His Royal Newburgh Assembly Rooms were built around this time and much of the Montpelier estate was his work – including the exquisite semi-detached Italianate-Regency houses of Montpelier Villas.

In 1830 Decimus Burton began the last great classical estate in Brighton. Forty-three years later, Palmeira Square was completed on the site of the monumental but short-lived Anthaeum, a giant glass house which collapsed on 30 August 1833. A comparison of Burton's original houses in Adelaide Crescent and those of Palmeira Square reflected the transition from the high Regency style to the more idiosyncratic Italianate vogue also evident in the grand avenues of the Cliftonville estate, built around the middle of the nineteenth century in what was then 'West Brighton' (and now Hove). With the extension of the new East Cliff sea wall to Kemp Town in 1838, the pieces of the classic Brighton and Hove sea front were locking into place.

Along that elegant front, the author of *A Day or Two at Brighton* (1852) observed how 'gentlemen on prancing steeds, and ladies in riding habits, are galloping about in all directions, probably in search of an appetite'. The trains were bringing in the visitors and the town was thronging from high summer to mid-winter. Of the many journals founded in the nineteenth century, the *Brighton Fashionable Visitors List* first appeared in July 1865: a replacement, perhaps, for

the now redundant Master of Ceremonies. Therein were recorded the names of titled aristocrats from Britain and abroad, and all the noble souls who, for twopence a time, could promenade on the Chain Pier, and enjoy its saloon and reading room, its regimental band, telescopes, silhouette artist, bazaar and the shops-within-the-towers which sold refreshments and trinkets. Was this a quaint foretaste of the Palace Pier as we know it today?

But by the 1840s fashionable society had already abandoned the Races to the more 'unsavoury elements'. The dreaded masses, who overturned *anciens régimes* in Europe and fuelled the Chartist crusade in England, were pouring in with every excursion train. The traditional St Bartholomew's Day Fair had become an excuse for 'drunkenness and debauchery', and residents complained that the town was awash with drunk and disorderly excursionists on Sundays. On Whit Sunday 1860 thirty-seven trains brought in some hundred and sixty thousand day-trippers. The town's need for its professional police force (established in 1838) was emphasized by the murder of Henry Solomon, the first chief of police, in 1844.

It was not only visitors who were (gradually) changing the face of Brighton. The population was exploding again. It rose by 41 per cent between 1841 and 1851. By 1861 the figure had increased from

. . . and Clifton Terrace

65,500 to 78,000. To Londoners in particular, the railway brought the possibility of a healthy life by the sea – for retired professionals and the first commuters. The railway also brought economic prosperity. The Brighton Railway Works were founded in 1842 and augmented by a locomotive manufacturing works in 1852. During the 'reign' of its celebrated superintendent, William Stroudley, Brighton Works employed over two thousand people. Undoubtedly, they contributed to the economic boom which fuelled the town's physical growth. And though Brighton held on to its radical reputation for some time to come, Chartist agitation was surely diluted by fuller employment.

Nevertheless, there was still much to be agitated about. The number of houses grew in direct ratio to the population. But while the well-to-do were able to afford the elegant villas of Cliftonville, 'the new suburb of Brighton' as it was described in 1859, and the middle-class estates of Clermont and Prestonville, which grew up in the 1860s, the lower orders were housed, as Brighton's famous sculptor Eric Gill put it, '[in] a congeries of more or less sordid streets, growing like a fungus' around the station and the railway works. And as the number of people and houses grew, so sanitation (to name but one) became more of a problem.

Brighton Railway Works –
with the London Road viaduct

There was much to concern the town's administrators. Too much, certainly, for the town commissioners, who came under increasing pressure from the proponents of incorporation. In December 1853 2,108 Brighton rate-payers petitioned the Queen's Privy Council for borough status. The following April Queen Victoria's charter of incorporation arrived in the town, which now, officially, adopted the name 'Brighton'. The first elections to the new council were held that May, and on 7 June 1854 Lt. Col. John Fawcett was created first mayor of the Municipal Borough of Brighton. The following year the town commissioners were officially disbanded. Control of the borough passed over to an elected body of thirty-six councillors and twelve aldermen, thereby ending any remaining influence of the old Hundred.

Guardians of the Poor, however, continued to be elected on a parochial rather than a municipal basis. Despite the national economic prosperity brought by the Industrial Revolution, by the middle of the nineteenth century there were more poor to guard than ever before. When Queen's Road was laid out in 1845 to provide better access from the station to North and West Streets, some of the immediate environs were improved: Air Street, for example – a notorious slum where once excrement from its several slaughterhouses festered in an open cesspit. The dwindling ranks of fishermen, and many of the town's servants, shop assistants and industrial workers often lived in abject squalor. Prosperity and a scarcity of land for building had forced up rents. Conditions in Brighton's slums were every bit as bad as those in the brick back-to-backs which supplied the dark satanic mills of the industrial North. Streets were dark and narrow; houses were small and grossly overcrowded, usually ill-ventilated and often riddled with damp. The

Cresy Report of 1849 had already exposed such blights as sewers running above basement level and cesspits adjacent to drinking wells – but nothing much was done. In 1860 government commissioners investigated Brighton, and their report told of 'deplorable drainage', an inadequate water supply and wells fouled by fetid refuse pits.

The report resulted in certain improvements. Between 1871 and 1874, for example, Sir John Hawkshaw designed and supervised a new 7 mile long sewer with an outfall at Portobello, 4 miles to the east of delicate Kemp Town noses. In the same decade, the corporation's first slum clearance scheme resulted in the demolition of Pimlico, Pym's Gardens and Orange Row. Collectively one of the worst areas of the North Laine, around one thousand inhabitants cohabited there with their livestock in 175 dwellings. From this area came Tom Sayers, the heroic bare-knuckle prize fighter who fought through forty-four gruelling rounds with the American, John Heenan, for a share of the world championship in 1860. But that, alas, is another story.

Such improvements, however, ultimately proved cosmetic. The mean streets of Victorian Brighton remained a breeding ground for vice and disease. Dr William Kebbell of the Brighton Dispensary had already (in 1848) exposed the link between squalor and such diseases as smallpox, scarlet fever, whooping-cough and consumption. Looking down on the town from the Downs, the author of *A Day or Two at Brighton* wrote of 'the city [pouring]

The Victorian workhouse – now Brighton's general hospital

forth from her thousand chimnies a volume of smoke that might almost rival "Auld Reekie" herself'. 'Like all great towns,' he observed, 'it has its comfortless, demoralized and poverty-stricken districts.' Their inhabitants often fell back on the traditional relief of alcohol. There were 479 pubs in 1859 – 774 in 1889! In the middle of the century the police were patrolling Edward Street in pairs, and a commentator of 1860 was describing 'hideous old women, drunken old men, and sometimes mere boys, hopelessly intoxicated, reeling and staggering' by night along Church Street.

But it was too convenient to claim that the demon alcohol was the cause of all the miseries of the 'lower orders'. In Victorian Britain any impulse for improvement, however, meant morals and charity. In 1872 the Brighton Charity Organization Society was founded to 'improve the condition of the poor, to administer relief, and to suppress begging'. Establishments like the Brighton, Hove and Preston Provident Dispensary gave out medical aid, while permanent soup kitchens dispensed sustenance – 126,493 quarts of it in 1843! The town outgrew its workhouse on Church Hill and, when the new building opened at the top of Elm Grove in 1867, the site was sold for development of more residential villas. Though the new workhouse became Brighton General Hospital in 1948, its foreboding exterior still summons up a regime which sanctioned one outing during the summer and one at Christmas. On the stairs of the Theatre Royal is a touching memento of that festive visit to the pantomime: an illustrated testimonial of thanks from the inmates for 'one of the few bright spots in the necessarily dull routine of workhouse life'. It was not deemed suitable for the children of paupers to share the dull routine of the adults. They were condemned to their own dull routine in the Warren Farm Industrial Schools, which opened in 1862 on land which later became part of Woodingdean.

Not all schools would have been quite so spartan. Such renowned private schools for the wealthy as Roedean and Brighton College opened during Victoria's reign. The railway helped to increase the number of boarding schools on the south coast; Brighton itself even acquired the moniker 'School Town'. Poorer children would have attended the charity schools and the increasing number of elementary schools founded by the church.

The church, of course, was a prime mover in the crusade against immorality. A judicial report of 1859 mentioned 325 known prostitutes, 25 of whom were under the age of 15. In reality the figure was probably twice that total. St Mary's Home for 'Female Penitents' (ex-prostitutes) was founded on a site opposite the Level in 1853. Eleven years later an employee of the new home in

THE "BRIGHTONIAN" CARTOON.

The Revd Arthur Wagner: high priest of Brighton's high church

Wykeham Terrace was linked with its new patron in a tale stranger than fiction. When Constance Kent stood trial for the murder of her young half-brother, the Revd Arthur Wagner's refusal to reveal her confession provoked an outcry – and an attempt on his life.

One of Brighton's most remarkable characters, Wagner was the son of the equally renowned Revd Henry Wagner. Together, the Wagners (soft 'w') financed a golden age of church building, thereby providing rent-free pews for the poor who were otherwise priced out of everywhere but St Peter's. In 1848 Wagner Sen. built St Paul's church in West Street for his son. His subsequent regret might be gleaned from a pointed paternal sermon from Matthew 17: 'Lord have mercy on my son for he is lunatic and sore vexed'. Parental disapproval focused on his son's conversion to the principles of the Oxford or Tractarian Movement and its crypto-Catholic 'High Church' ritualism: a reaction to the rise of non-conformist worship during more liberal Regency times. 'Beautiful ceremony, singing and furnishings' were, in the words of Sir John Betjeman, the hallmarks of the 'London, Brighton and South Coast religion'. Brighton had its fair share of religious demagogues: Henry James Prince declared himself and his followers immortal in the 1840s, and John William Wood proclaimed himself 'King Solomon' in 1887 and briefly cast out devils from his Sanctuary of Jehovah in Edward Street. But, for all the derision and calumny the Revd Arthur Wagner suffered in the name of his beliefs, he was no mere populist. He is remembered as much for his extraordinary generosity to the poor as for the Constance Kent affair. Once mocked as 'Wagner's folly', the

St Bartholomew's: towering like Noah's Ark over London Road

most lasting monument to his religion still towers over London Road. Opened in 1874 and built to the dimensions of Noah's Ark, St Bartholomew's is said to be the highest church in the land.

For all this philanthropy, for all the temperance societies and 'coffee houses', the Church could not compete with Victorian gin houses – even though the Clayton Tunnel disaster of 25 August 1861 seemed a 'moral judgement from heaven' on the evils of Sunday excursions. Nor could it fundamentally improve living conditions for the increasingly numerous poor of the parish. It seems that only when disease and squalor threatened to damage Brighton's salutary reputation did rate-payers mobilize for action. In one week in June 1882, they raised £6,000 – for public relations. The media came to the rescue to refute the damaging critiques published in *The Lancet* and save the coming bathing season. 'In thee we will not lose our faith,' declaimed *Society Magazine*, 'Queen of the Sea'.

And though times had changed, Brighton was still the marine queen. By 1886 there were over a hundred doctors in Brighton and Hove, but the sea was no longer seen as a medical cure. Bathing was now merely a healthy pursuit, while the new medical sciences of 'climatology' and 'medical topography' shifted the focus to the benefits of sea air. Sir James Clark, Dr Edwin Lee, Dr William Kebbell and others professed to identify micro-climates within the town, each suiting certain categories of patients. With the emphasis on pure, invigorating sea air, the passion to promenade became all-consuming. King's Road was widened on several occasions to accommodate the carriages and pedestrians. Madeira Drive was built in 1872, and its popularity as a promenade was enhanced with the building of a ¾ mile long terrace between 1890 and 1897, along with a hydraulic lift to Marine Parade above and a hall providing shelter during inclement weather. The opening of Eugenius Birch's West Pier in 1866 and the new concrete groynes offered alternative promenades over the sea. There were moonlight promenades after the concerts and Sundays witnessed the church parade: a display of dress, wealth and, to quote the contemporary press, 'the daintiest books of common prayer'.

Display was still the thing, and a correspondent of *The Graphic* counted '274 carriages and vehicles entirely devoted to pleasure' passing the bottom of West Street during a ten-minute period one November day in 1873. But the genus of 'displayer' was evolving. The middle classes began to mingle more with the upper classes as respectability became the password to the promenade. Were the popular goat carriages which operated on the lower esplanade conscious miniatures of those which passed above? Certainly theory suggests that parks were created to tempt the lower orders out of doors, there to mimic their betters instead of slaking their thirsts in public houses.

The new show hotels from the West Pier

Two of Brighton's finest were opened to the public in the latter years of Victoria's reign: Preston Park in 1883 and Queen's Park in 1892.

In such a class-conscious society, it was appropriate that the lower orders gravitated towards the lower esplanade and the beach itself (though free bathing was only permitted from certain designated public bathing places between certain hours). By 1880 there were 150 ladies' and 100 gentlemen's bathing machines on Brighton beach, and indoor establishments like Brill's Baths were still popular. For the poor, however, bathing might have meant a personal bath at one of the council-built public slipper baths. The two societies of Victorian England rarely met. The *Fin de Siècle Review* of 1897 boasted that 'Brighton possesses the largest number of hotels . . . and residential establishments, to be found on an area of equal extent in the world' to accommodate the 'vast army of visitors'. But only the better-heeled would have stayed at the great new show hotels of the front: the Norfolk Resort (1864–6), for example, or the eight-storey Grand (1862–4) with its 150 bedrooms and miraculous 'ascending omnibus', or the largest (and ugliest, according to critics of the time), Alfred Waterhouse's red-brick and terracotta Metropole (1890). The lodging-house keepers, satirized as 'vultures' and 'crocodiles', would have preyed on poorer passers-by.

59

For entertainment, the 'rank-and-file' had their back-room public house shows, known as 'penny gaffs', and early music halls. Though the great balls of Regency days were a thing of the past, rank and respectability still had its dances and concerts, and a Theatre Royal flourishing under the management of first Nye and then Nellie Chart. The closure of the Albion Rooms in 1869 and the loss of the Old Ship Assembly Rooms to an auction house in 1885 were compensated by the transformation of the royal stables into a resplendent concert hall known as the Dome, and the establishment of such genteel social venues as the famous Mutton's Hotel and Restaurant on King's Road – and the Aquarium. Built at great expense on the approach road to the Chain Pier, and opened in 1872, this vast underground extravaganza, with its marine exhibits, reading room, restaurant, resident orchestra, organ recitals, military bands and concert artists, soon proved a resounding commercial success.

The Aquarium's extraordinary Winter Garden

So, Brighton continued to grow. The population increased from 90,000 in 1871 to 115,000 in 1891. Steadily, the town expanded northwards: the Lewes Road combe became a largely artisan preserve, while the sale of large parts of the Stanford estate, from 1871 on, provided land for the middle-class properties which spread along and up the London Road combe as far now as Preston. Hove, meanwhile, was growing at an even faster rate.

Magnus Volk's 'Daddy Long-legs' powers past the East Cliff – at 2 m.p.h.!

A new century was dawning and times were changing. Not only the inhabitants, but also the hotels, shops and service industries demanded modern facilities. A gas supply had been long established; in 1872 the corporation took control of the water supply; and, in 1882, the world's first permanent public electricity service was supplied (before takeover by the corporation in 1894) by Robert Hammond's Electric Light and Power company. Consumers were warned not to strike matches to light the new bulbs!

A pioneer of electricity was Brighton's celebrated inventor, Magnus Volk. In 1883 he installed a power supply in the Royal Pavilion and its grounds. That same year his electric railway opened on the sea front. In 1896 the Rottingdean Seashore Electric Railway was opened, and Volk's extraordinary 'Daddy Long-legs' further transformed the sea front scene. This four-legged mechanical creation was said to have provided H.G. Wells with a futuristic image for *War of the Worlds*. Its brief but troubled life was disrupted by such events as the great storm of December 1896, which wrecked the ailing Chain Pier. How appropriate that such a potent symbol of a bygone age should be swept away at the turn of a century and replaced by an equally potent symbol of a more egalitarian age to come. It took eight years to build the Palace Pier, but when it was opened at last in the summer of 1899, it proved an immediate

A unique view of all three piers

success. More 'down-market' than its older cousin to the west, the new pier catered for the holiday crowds of a new epoch.

The railway bringeth and the railway taketh away. . . . The 1890s witnessed a comparative decline in Brighton's fortunes as an expanding railway network now enabled the town's former patrons to head further south in the winter – to Rome or the south of France. But, on 14 November 1896, thirty-three motor cars set off from Hyde Park for the Metropole Hotel, to celebrate their emancipation from the man with the red flag. A new age of communications would soon create a whole new set of changes. . . .

CHAPTER SEVEN

The Cockney Paradise

Dip me in the sea at Brighton
London by the Sea –
That's the place for me.

from *Sunshine Girl* (1912)

The crowd is very dense, and paper and litter are strewn about in such large quantities as almost to suggest a snowstorm.

from *Two Days in Brighton* (1925)

T hanks to the railway, Brighton was little more than an hour away from London. An anonymous author of 1862 had caricatured the Sunday excursionists of 'the "London Ordinary", a magnificent apartment under the cliff, having for its carpet the countless pebbles of the seashore, and for its roof the vaulted sky'. And, of course, London was little more than an hour away from the coast. The 'stock-jobbers' who, according to William Cobbett in 1823, 'skip backward and forward on the coaches', were few in number, but the railways now conveyed a considerable phalanx of commuters to the capital and back. In 1851 *Knight's Excursion Companion* suggested that 'we might . . . almost class Brighton as a suburb of the metropolis'.

Fashionable promenaders had already sniffed the insidious influence of London and abandoned first the beach and then the town itself to a new breed of visitor. In 1900 the Royal Albion had closed. The Royal York was deserted. In 1901 the council sanctioned mixed bathing (from machines only) and took over the ailing Aquarium. Property values were falling; in 1903 Lord Rendell acquired twenty or so of the great Kemp Town houses and began the trend of converting them into flats. The writing appeared to be on the wall.

But Brighton's history is one of resilience and adaptability. Society was indeed changing: enlightened legislation such as the Workmen's

Compensation Act of 1906 and the Old Age Pensions Act of 1909 were sowing seeds of a more equal era. By riding rather than bucking the trend, the town ensured more good times just around the corner. In 1909 Lewis Melville lamented that 'Brighton is interesting only in its past. . . . Brighton has developed into the Cockney's Paradise, the Mecca of the stockbroker and the chorus girl. . . . The town now boasts mammoth hotels and theatres and music-halls in all parts and you may now obtain everything but quiet.' He may not have liked it, but there were plenty who did. It was precisely that bustle and variety which secured Brighton's future; in the twentieth century, it became a place which could offer almost everything that the capital could, and one thing more besides. The sea.

As with the advent of the railways, however, change was not cemented overnight. In fact, the years of Edward VII's reign witnessed an 'Indian summer of fashionability'. It was, admittedly, a different kind of fashionability: one founded not just on rank or title, but also on wealth, fame, even notoriety. As ever, certain individual lights burned brightly enough to attract the high-flyers. One of them was Harry Preston: a charismatic little man who sported a carnation and smoked ten large Havana cigars a day. A genial ex-boxer, he was blessed with a rare business acumen and a gift for publicity helped by his own marketable passions for boxing, motor yachts, motor cars and aeroplanes. Moving east from Bournemouth, he purchased first the Royal York (in 1901) and later the Royal Albion (1913), restored their fame and fortune (and sold the former to the council in 1929 for a considerable profit).

While staying at the Royal York, Arnold Bennett wrote *Clayhanger*. His novel of 1910 describes the town during its Indian summer, when colourful crowds were pulled in by Preston's promotions. In 1905, for instance, he was a prime mover behind the first motor speed-trials held on Madeira Drive, one of the first roads in the country to be surfaced by tarmacadam. The presence of Rolls, Brabazon, Guinness and other renowned enthusiasts, and the setting of record speeds, created a blaze of publicity. The subsequent daring feats of pioneer aviators helped to fan this blaze. In 1910 Preston flew the roof-tops with the aviator, André Beaumont, in a reconstructed Blériot monoplane. The following year the flying ground at nearby Shoreham was opened officially as Brighton Aerodrome. In 1913 a sea-plane station was established at the Banjo Groyne. What with the aerobatic stunts and unofficial landings (on Roedean's hockey field, for instance) and the aerial races, the years just before the First World War must have been golden ones for local journalists. Preston's own hotels – indeed, all of Brighton's luxury hotels – were prospering again from the influx of rich and famous

Another Preston promotion:
the 1905 speed trials

clients. His knighthood in 1930 was just reward for services rendered to his adopted town.

A family of rich merchants also served as catalysts. Pre-eminent among a significant Jewish population, which had come to settle in Brighton and Hove, were the Sassoons. Their guests included the Rothschilds – and King Edward VII. As Prince of Wales, he had visited Brighton on a number of occasions: in 1865, for example, he had come down for the annual volunteer soldier reviews, which brought the Easter crowds to Race Hill for many years. Between 1908 and 1910 he made several visits for the sake of his health, and his favourite venue appeared to be No. 8, King's Gardens, Hove: the home of Arthur Sassoon. Edward's visits proved a resounding success. 'Nothing', suggested the *Brighton Herald* in 1908, 'could be more calculated to bring about an influx of rank and fashion to the town.' They may not have helped his health much, since Edward VII died in 1910, but his visits certainly brought the crowds: in August 1909 they were reputedly the biggest ever seen. The Sunday morning promenade thronged as never before. In commemoration (and gratitude?), the eastern part of Brighton's sea front was renamed King's Cliff, while Hove's front was christened Kingsway.

The crowds came by rail and by road. Improvements to the line had reduced the journey by certain trains to an hour or less. In 1905 the first of the famous Sunny South Specials brought holidaymakers from Liverpool and Manchester. At the other end of the social spectrum, November 1908 saw the introduction of the self-styled 'most luxurious train in the world', the Southern (later, Brighton) Belle service. There was increasing activity on the roads now: open-top charabancs (described by Sid Manville in his *mémoires* of *A Brighton Boyhood Between the Wars* as 'enormous painted meat-baking tin[s] on wheels') provided an early coach service for as little as 4 s. for a day return from London to Brighton; and, although the old horse-drawn mail coaches were finally phased out in 1905, the American millionaire Alfred G. Vanderbilt sponsored an unlikely stage-coach revival. Both the 'Venture' and the 'Viking' ran between London and Brighton every summer until 1914, but their splendid teams of horses and fashionable passengers brought more spectators than profits. On at least one occasion, King Edward himself chose to make the journey by private car. There were sufficient numbers of cars on the road to warrant the founding of an Automobile Association. Initially, its sole function seemed to be that of warning motorists on the London to Brighton road of police speed-traps!

Though the advent of the First World War in August 1914 dampened this 'Indian summer of fashionability', the *Brighton &*

Catering for vast numbers of the 'typical crowd'

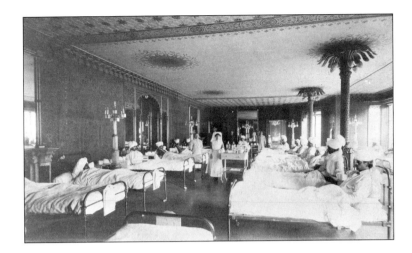

Glimpses of Nirvana: the
Pavilion as a hospital for
wounded Indian soldiers

Hove Gazette's prediction that 'the restrictions on continental traffic should increase the rush to English pleasure resorts' was to prove correct. While the 1907 *Who's Who in Hove* could boast that 'this town never has its serenity disturbed by the incursion of beanfeasters, half-holiday people, or the typical summer crowd', Brighton thrived on its ability to cater for vast numbers of this typical crowd. During the war years, the crowd was typically varied, and featured rich refugees from London and Europe, politicians (even Lloyd George himself), and war profiteers. The town's hotels and theatres prospered, and the Municipal Orchestra played all the year round.

Brighton also gave back to the war effort. The railway works, which had earlier shown signs of decline, made a considerable contribution to war-time production. The Pavilion, too, had a major role to play. Despite the return of some of its plundered treasures, over-painting and varnishing had contributed to what Mrs John Lane described in 1907 as the 'shabby worn-out appearance of an old impecunious rake'. At the suggestion of George V, the Royal Pavilion and the Dome were converted into a military hospital. With a delicious, if unconscious, *coup de théâtre*, it became an exotic refuge for wounded soldiers of the Indian army. Before it was given over to the limbless during the second half of the war, 4,306 Indian patients were treated between November 1914 and February 1916 – and this despite the difficulties of catering for religious and caste systems which necessitated nine different kitchens and two distinct supplies of water. There are poignant tales of soldiers coming round from anaesthetic and staring at the decor in the mistaken belief that they were now in paradise. Those who didn't make it were cremated in a ceremonial ghat, whose site is marked by the Chattri erected, in 1921, to their memory on the Downs at Patcham.

The same year a new south gate to the Pavilion grounds was built as a gift to the town from the people of India.

The gift to Britain's own soldiers, returning from the bloody theatre of war, was to be in the form of 'homes fit for heroes'. The slums of Victorian Brighton, however, were not razed over-night. Indeed, Graham Greene's *Brighton Rock* (1938) and John Boulting's subsequent film version paint a dim picture of the town between the wars. So how accurate, how fair was this picture of dingy back streets and vicious razor gangs?

Seeking to elude Pinky and his thugs, Hale tries to lose himself in the crowd. 'Fifty thousand people besides himself were down for the day.' The crowds may have glittered less than they did in pre-war days, but the 'London Ordinary' kept coming down in vast numbers. Residents recall the days when the dense queues to the station stretched down Queen's Road to the clock tower and beyond. They still talk of the mass post-breakfast exodus from side-street boarding houses to beaches where people swarmed like ants to the water's edge, until the fanfare of gongs summoned them back to the dining rooms. Southern Railway statistics speak of two-and-a-half million passengers entering Brighton during the nine weeks ending 9 September 1925. In August 1928 a record number of 623 motor coaches arrived in one day.

The novel only hints at the sheer diversity of entertainments on offer. In *Two Days in Brighton* (1925), the anonymous author gets carried away in a torrent of extravagant hyperbole. The combination of Queen's Road and West Street, with its 'gin palaces, . . . sausage and mashed [sic] establishments, . . . auction rooms and . . . fun palaces' is described as the 'Piccadilly of the Queen City' (ranking with Prince's Street in Edinburgh and the Rue de la Paix in Paris!), while Brighton itself 'is quite as brilliant as Monte Carlo, Nice or Cairo, only of course in a different way'. He writes of the market of stalls between the piers 'reminiscent of Algiers' and the happy-jackers: the crowds of young kids on the lower esplanade who would urge passers-by to drop sticks of rock and pennies from the promenade above. He talks of evening open-air dances on the West Pier. What with all the troops of entertainers and minstrel shows and bands playing day and night, the air must have hummed with music. The 1920 *Guide Book* was still advertising 'Brighton for Health and Pleasure', and there were ample salubrious pursuits on offer: one could travel by charabanc or the branch-line railway to Devil's Dyke, or partake in the Edwardian passion for paddle-steamers. The *Brighton Belle* and its sister vessels offered trips from the piers to Worthing, the Isle of Wight, even Boulogne.

Above all, there was the variety show. Brighton was second only to London in the variety of live entertainment on offer. The 'penny

''Allo missus!' The 'cheeky chappie' himself, mean Max Miller

Brighton's principal variety theatre in its heyday

A Theatre Royal programme boasts its London connections

gaffs' and early music halls had already established its flowering variety tradition. Fred Ginnett, an ex-circus artist, founded the Gaiety and Eden (later the Grand) Theatres towards the end of the nineteenth century, and by the early years of the next one the Hippodrome had opened and the pavilions of both piers had been converted into theatres. Edwardians could have paid to see the likes of Charlie Chaplin at the Hippodrome, Harry Tate at the Alhambra or Houdini at the Arcadia Theatre of Varieties. After the war Sherry's opened on the same site where eighteenth-century literati gathered under the roof of Henry and Hester Thrales. Along with the Hippodrome, it would dominate Brighton's nightlife during the inter-war years with bills featuring international stars like Jack Hylton, Louis Armstrong, Duke Ellington, Fats Waller and Cab Calloway, touring reviews and, of course, the 'cheeky chappie' himself, Max Miller. Like many others, he served his apprenticeship in the summer season concert parties. Such hardy perennials as Jack Shepherd's Entertainers must have transformed the front into one big variety show.

At any time during the 1930s no less than six theatres were operating in Brighton. While the Palace Pier Theatre staged touring plays, musical comedies, concerts, pierrot shows, circuses and pantomimes in its large Moorish-style auditorium, the West Pier Theatre tended to present 'straight' theatre along the lines of the Theatre Royal, whose 'flying matinées' during the reign of the Charts developed into rather longer-term links with the West End. Noël Coward, for one, often tried out his new pieces there and during 1936 twenty-six West End shows 'tested the waters' at Brighton's premier theatre. Most major stars of the day would have appeared on some Brighton stage at some time.

And so a resident artistic colony flourished during this age of popular entertainments. Stars of stage and screen settled by the sea. The turn of the century had witnessed the birth of British film production on the coast, with a Brighton school growing up around such pioneers of the moving picture as William Friese-Greene, Esme Collings (whose catalogue included blue films 'for gentlemen only'), Alfred Darling and two Hove photographers: George Albert Smith and James Williamson. St Anne's Well Gardens in Hove became the venue for Charles Urban's first purpose-built film studio. Then, after the war, Progress Films produced at least thirty films from a base in Shoreham, including *Moving a Piano* featuring Charlie Chaplin. During the 1920s, 'Bohemia-on-Sea' grew up on Shoreham Beach around such contemporary stars as Marie Lloyd, Anna Pavlova, Jack Hulbert, Cicely Courtneidge and Lupino Lane. The community achieved notoriety not just for its wild parties and brilliant nightlife, but also for its bizarre residences. Horse boxes and railway carriages became homes fit for eccentrics, and houses were built in the shape of a ship, an ark, a Chinese pagoda, even a matchbox.

Hell's Angel gate-crashes Brighton's 'largest and finest Kinematographic establishment'!

Little wonder then, that the cinema should feature so prominently in Brighton's inter-war menu of entertainments. From 1937 to 1939 there were seventeen cinemas in Brighton. And these were not just any old cinemas: this was the era of the 'Super Cinemas'. The Regent was built in 1921 on the corner of North Street and Queen's Road. With its giant auditorium, its restaurant, cafe and a roof-top garden which was later converted into a dance-hall, this 'gorgeous temple of the silent drama' was described by the *Brighton Herald* as 'the largest, finest Kinematographic establishment in the country if not in the entire world'. In 1930 the huge Art Deco Savoy opened on the site of today's Cannon in East Street; three years later The Astoria opened in Gloucester Place. It is symptomatic of changing times and changing pastimes that the former should have been built on the site of Brill's Baths, while the latter became a bingo emporium in 1977.

The money was there for cinemas – the Regent, for example, cost £400,000 to build – but, until the government offered financial subsidies for slum clearance schemes in 1930, it wasn't there for housing. The fascinating oral histories of these times published by QueenSpark books tell tales of squalor and deprivation: in 1921, for example, Brighton was, after West Ham in London, the most densely populated borough in the country. But entertainment was cheap, cheerful and diverse, and an antidote to hard times. Above all, these books tell tales of remarkable fortitude and resourcefulness, of people smiling in the face of adversity. For Brighton's poor the inter-war years were times of long hours and low pay, pawn shops and means tests, big families and stern discipline, bed bugs, nits and hair inspections, flying

'The shabby secret behind the bright corsage' (Carlton Court)

visits from the sanitary man, daughters condemned to service at the age of fourteen, scraps of food and such long-lost diseases as scarlet fever, rickets, whooping-cough, diphtheria and consumption. But then, they were also times of crowded back streets enriched by the sight of lamplighters, the smell of herrings smoking on 'dees', the sound of musicians and street singers, and the cries of knife-grinders, ice-cream vendors, barrow boys and kids at play. Greene's description of back street Brighton as 'the shabby secret behind the bright corsage' is memorable, but his anti-hero is excluded from the potent spirit of community to which these oral histories testify. In *Backyard Brighton* Bert Nelson talks of life in the condemned Gerrard's Court as 'one of utter bliss. . . . The Court seemed to be all protecting and we were a little colony not caught up in the outside world.'

It was, it would seem, an era of the caring, sharing community. Though the workhouse system was ended and the Board of Guardians was dissolved in 1930, other well-meaning guardians of the borough began the process of dismantling it. Ruby Dunn's *Moulsecoomb Days* describes the establishment of a new community on virgin land to the east of the Lewes Road, acquired by the corporation in 1920. The 478 houses which constituted the model garden estate of South Moulsecoomb were intended as new homes for residents of the Carlton Hill area, dispossessed by the first of the post-war slum clearances in 1923. However, the corporation's rents were too high, and many of the new tenants or owners came from London and other towns, enticed by a florid advertising campaign.

For several years there were no communal amenities to speak of, and Ruby Dunn's autobiography tells of epic walks to and from school. Facilities only came as the estate was extended into North Moulsecoomb and up the Bevendean valley over the next decade or so. As the slum clearance programme gathered steam in the 1930s, the East Brighton council estates at Whitehawk and Manor Farm were built, while the Milner and Kingswood flats sprang up on the site of the demolished slums. But, as one of the contributors to *Backstreet Brighton* describes, better living standards sometimes offered no compensation for the break-up of a close community: 'My mother got Moulsecoomb, and my aunt, who lived opposite, got Woodingdean. They weren't kept together, they didn't put any thought into it at all.' Looking today at some of the properties which might have been condemned, seeing how grants and tender loving care can transform them into desirable residences, only underlines how misguided a well-meaning policy could be.

The new garden suburb of South Moulsecoomb – intended for residents of Carlton Hill

So, little was done to alleviate conditions for the poor of Brighton until the 1930s. During the previous decade self-help and direct action were the orders of the day. The resurgence of the Cooperative movement culminated in the opening of a department store in London Road – today the largest in Brighton. And a bowler-hatted chimney sweep by the name of Harry Cowley became a folk hero for his tireless crusades on behalf of the unemployed or the 'barrow boys'. 'The Guv'nor', as he became known, helped to establish permanent market sites in Upper Gardner Street and opposite the Level. His 'vigilantes' stirred up controversy by promoting squatting as one solution to the housing problem. During the General Strike of 1926, however, it was the other bowler-hatted Harry, namely Harry Preston, who hit the headlines. His mounted force of Volunteer Specials helped to break up a four thousand plus crowd which had gathered outside the tram depot in Lewes Road to demonstrate against strike-breakers. Although the *Herald* proclaimed 'A victory of common sense over Moscow inspired illusion', the savagery with which the crowd was dispersed left a stain known as the Battle of Lewes Road.

Brighton Rock's concentration on the violent aspects of the resort was not without foundation. The corporation had taken over the Races at the peak of their popularity in 1888, and spent some £60,000 on improvements to the course in the 1930s. Nevertheless, the vicious protection rackets operated by London-based razor gangs made the headlines at the expense of the side-shows described by Bert Healey in his *Hard Times and Easy Terms*: the food stalls, the hurdy-gurdies, the traders, 'Prince Monolulu' and his brethren of colourful tipsters, the coconut shies and other fairground attractions. Only when the police broke up the thirty-strong 'Hoxton Mob' at Lewes Races in June 1936

Was *Brighton Rock* good for the town?

was peace restored. But Brighton had already been dubbed 'the queen of slaughtering places' thanks to two lurid crimes, known collectively as the Brighton Trunk Murders, which dominated the newspapers in the summer of 1934. The case of the dismembered female torso found in a trunk at Brighton station was to remain unsolved; and nearly forty years later Toni Mancini confessed to the *News of the World* that he had murdered Violette Kaye and hidden her body in the other trunk, a crime for which he had been acquitted at the time.

The Brighton of Greene's novel was a considerably larger town. The growth in population to 147,427 in 1931 reflected an expansion of the boundaries. On 1 April 1928 'Greater Brighton' was created. The fortunes of Patcham, like Preston, had long been linked to the resort's: an older agrarian way of life had already given way to intensive market gardening and dairy production in the face of demand for supplies from a burgeoning Victorian town. Most of the parish was now officially annexed by Brighton, along with parts or all of Falmer, West Blatchington, Ovingdean and Rottingdean. Between 1923 and 1928 therefore, Brighton grew by almost 10,000 acres. The parish of Rottingdean by now incorporated Saltdean: one part of a speculator's dream to develop all the land between Rottingdean and Newhaven. Charles Neville never quite fulfilled that dream. Once dismissed as 'a clever fraud', Peacehaven nevertheless commemorates Neville's brazen tenacity.

The new northern boundary was marked by Brighton's famous stone pylons on the A23 to London. Their cost was borne largely by Sir Herbert Carden, the 'maker of modern Brighton'. A wealthy solicitor, Carden was associated with the council for over forty years. He advocated the policy of land purchase, and by 1936 a further 7,000 acres within and 5,000 acres outside the new boundaries had been bought to create a green belt, safeguard a natural amenity for the people of Brighton, preserve the water supply and/or provide land for municipal housing. Carden himself bought land at Hollingbury and the Devil's Dyke, and resold it at cost to the corporation.

It was motor transport – the car and the bus – which made communal settlement of the new hinterland a possibility. Similarly, it was motor transport which helped to lift the face of Brighton's centre. Between the wars, the council spent around £2 million on slum clearance and road-widening. The bottle-neck known as 'The Dawkins Dardanelles', for example, was eradicated as Western Road was widened in the 1930s and fitted with such notable stores as the Boots building of 1928. During the depression years large sums of money were also spent in just enabling Brighton to keep up with its rivals. The Aquarium was rebuilt in 1929. The construction of the Undercliff Walk between Black Rock and Rottingdean provided employment for up to five hundred men between 1930 and 1933. At around the same time Marine Drive, a 60-ft highway, was built to replace the original road linking Marine Parade to Rottingdean. In 1935 the giant municipal rock garden was laid out opposite Preston Park. That same year redecoration of the Royal Pavilion reflected critical reappraisal; and the Dome – previously the venue for Harry Preston's boxing promotions – was refurbished for its new role as the town's leading concert and conference centre. Further improvements were made to the sewage system, and a feature of the Brighter Brighton policy was the wholesale removal of unsightly railings.

Brighton and Hove already had a football team, and a county cricket club enjoying halcyon days; with the opening of the Withdean stadium in 1936, it now also had the finest tennis centre outside Wimbledon. Public swimming pools were opened at Rottingdean in 1935, Black Rock in 1936 and Saltdean in 1937, where Richard Jones's gleaming Lido proclaimed the influence of the celebrated De la Warr Pavilion in Bexhill. The £80,000 investment in, reputedly, the largest covered pool in the world looked doomed when SS Brighton (so called because the interior was made to look like an ocean-going liner) closed in the same year it opened. But it reopened the following year, 1935, as a sports stadium and played host to ice shows and

'Open air dancing.' During the 1930s everyone came to Brighton

sports such as ice hockey. Its most famous tenants, the Brighton Tigers ice hockey team, were to find glory soon after the next war.

No doubt Sir Herbert Carden's influence in all this was prominent. Certainly he was behind such municipal enterprises as the tram and telephone systems. His bold spirit of innovation surely rubbed off on a council which, nationally, was to take the lead in providing pedestrian crossings and equipping its police with radio receivers. Fortunately, though, certain aspects of Carden's vision were never realized. During the 1930s roof extensions and wholesale conversions into mansion flats combined to damage the architectural purity of the great houses of the sea front. Then, in 1935, Wells Coates built his aggressively modern Embassy Court next door to the classic Brunswick Terrace. To Carden, the town's first high-rise block of exclusive flats 'show[ed] the way'. He wanted to replace all the buildings on the front with a string of Embassy Courts. He wanted to 'scrap the Pavilion' as 'a complete anachronism in a modern age'. And he wanted to demolish the Lanes.

Showing the way? Embassy Court sits in the middle of a classic sea front

For the time being, though, Brighton's aesthetic sanctity was preserved. And so, too, despite *Brighton Rock* and all the bad publicity, was the resort's popularity. Throughout the 1930s Brighton's appeal cut through class barriers. Everyone came to Brighton. In any one year during the decade, that meant around ten million day trippers and a further half million longer stay visitors. Everyone was determined to have a good time and everyone, it seemed, wanted to dance: at Sherry's, at the Regent Ballroom, at the Savoy Cinema, at the Aquarium, on the piers, even at Boot's new store. The town was a veritable cockneys' paradise.

On the August Bank Holiday of 1939 forty-five thousand visitors were lured to the Palace Pier by its beauty contests, its fancy dress contests, its bicycle divers and follies and slot machines, its cafés and restaurants and military band. A few days later, war broke out. Coastal defences went up; the black-out was enforced. Twenty-three Brighton vessels crossed the Channel to help in the Dunkirk evacuation; two of the famous Collins family's *Skylarks* and three of the town's paddle steamers were sunk. Hitler's troops were anticipated daily during August and September 1940. To protect the town against 'Operation Sealion', the beach was mined and wired, and gaps blown in the two piers. Lord Haw-Haw had it that Hitler intended to make the Royal Pavilion his headquarters. . . .

CHAPTER EIGHT

A Delicate Balance

The old world as we knew it before the war with its privileged and leisured classes is doomed, and a belief in its return is sheer delusion.

Dr Bell, Bishop of Chichester (1942)

We believe that a proper balance can be achieved, and that constructive consultation and criticism can help in achieving it.

From the Aims of the Brighton Society

H ad 'Operation Sealion' taken place, Brighton might well have been blown to bits. Four to five thousand troops were scheduled to land on its beaches. As it was, Brighton was right in the firing line during the Second World War. Between July 1940 and March 1944 the town suffered 56 air raids in which 198 people were killed and 280 houses were totally destroyed. The Black Rock gas works received a direct hit, the railway works were partially destroyed and

Right in the firing line

the London Road viaduct was seriously damaged. Bombs fell in the Pavilion grounds: they missed the palace itself, but shook the Dome's walls out of the vertical. Miraculously, though, the vast majority of the town's architectural treasures were spared.

Brighton was no haven for evacuees. The thousands who poured in during the days of the 'phoney war' were subsequently 're-evacuated'. For most of the war Brighton was labelled a 'defence zone' and had to live with a ban on visitors: barbed wire protected its beaches from storm-troopers and its boundaries from day-trippers. Not that the town's entertainments industry shut down completely. When Brighton became a focus for the allied invasion, the huge influx of American and Canadian troops resuscitated the old Queen.

At the end of the war Brighton celebrated in a style befitting its former royal patron. During the VJ Day festivities, deck chairs and beach huts helped stoke the sea front bonfires. The town had had a most fortunate escape. How ironic, then, that a new and different war was already fermenting: a war between the forces of change and the forces of conservation; a war which was to inflict more damage on the town than the forces of Nazi Germany.

The very same year that the war ended, 1945, Hove council announced plans to redevelop its sea front. The plans involved the demolition of Brunswick Square and Terrace, and Adelaide Crescent. In their place, the progressives proposed high-rise flats and a car park! The proposals raised a storm of protest: D.L. Murray published an influential article in *The Times*, and he and three other like-minded individuals – Antony Dale, Clifford Musgrave and Sir William Teeling – convened a public meeting in the banqueting room of the Royal Pavilion on 11 December 1945. From that historic meeting the Regency Society was born, with Dale its treasurer and Musgrave its secretary. Its published aim was to 'awaken appreciation of [Brighton and Hove's] rich architectural heritage and to stimulate interest in the art and architecture of the Georgian, Regency and Victorian periods'. The two opposing forces had names now: on one side, the planners; on the other, the conservationists. The plans were dropped. First blood to the forces of conservation.

During the war the Pavilion had been put to work for town and country. The cellars, for example, were used as air-raid shelters and corporation pigsties were set up in the grounds outside the King's Apartments. Now the Regency Society put it to work for them – as a venue for exhibitions and three Regency Festivals between 1946 and 1951. Membership of the society grew, and it achieved a significant victory in persuading Hove Corporation to use the colour 'Regency cream' for the triannual repainting of Brunswick's stucco.

Some of many that missed the list – William Street and Edward Street were redeveloped after the war

In the wake of the Brunswick proposals, the society compiled a list of all the buildings in the twin boroughs which were of special significance. In 1952 a list of 647 'buildings of architectural and historical interest', classed in Grades I and II, was certified by the Minister of Housing and Local Government. A supplementary list categorized a further 876 as Grade III. Brighton, like every other planning authority, was obliged by the same minister to prepare a development plan for approval. The accompanying report stated that its prime object was to 'strengthen the attractions of Brighton as a coastal resort without sacrificing its character'. But so toothless was the legislation, that the development plan was able to substitute a much abbreviated list of 'buildings recommended for preservation' with impunity. Many of the buildings listed by the minister, it reported, were 'such that it would be quite contrary to the public interest to preserve them'.

Initial post-war plans and proposals only suggest confusion in the ranks of the town's municipal masters. Did they envisage another Blackpool or a kind of Bath-on-Sea? Such confusion is evident in the decision to move the fish market from the front to a site where the smell of herrings would not offend visitors. Flora Robson reputedly used to buy her fish from the Fish Market Hard and if it was good enough for her, then it was certainly good enough for visitors attracted, no doubt, by just this strange combination of gentility and vulgarity. Writing in 1895, G.A. Sala had urged that 'Brighton must preserve its ancestral character as a place whither people of every degree repair to get well and be amused'.

For the time being, at least, people were doing just that. The immediate post-war years witnessed another boom. The new Labour government's legislation provided for additional paid annual holidays for the nation's work force. Starved of holidays for the last six years, Londoners and the like flocked back to the south coast. The piers were repaired and the illuminations were restored. The town still had five theatres and sufficient cinemas to provide one seat for every seven residents. There were concert parties and candyfloss, and the beaches were crowded once more.

But the boom didn't last. Brighton, like every other resort, suffered from competition with the new holiday camps. Increased car ownership meant increased opportunities for touring holidays. The smallpox epidemic of 1950–1 damaged Brighton's image. Soon, the era of the teenager would inflict further harm, with first teddy boys, then beatniks, and then mods and rockers presenting reasons for the traditional tripper to stay away. Just across the horizon, there was the additional threat of the package holiday to Spain and elsewhere.

The business of predicting and responding to post-war trends, which were becoming ever more fickle and volatile, must have been a difficult one for the council. And the interests it had to satisfy often conflicted. On the one hand, there were those demanding added attractions for day-trippers – and, although plans to invest £1 million in a giant pleasure beach and to build a fun fair and scenic railway in the Roedean area were shelved, Peter Pan's Playground was

Mods and rockers busy damaging Brighton's image

built on reclaimed land between the Palace Pier and Black Rock. On the other hand, however, there were those demanding better housing, hospitals and schools. Large new housing estates were built at Hollingdean and Hollingbury. In 1947 the corporation bought the Stanmer estate: 4,958 acres of woodland, which included the villages of Stanmer and Falmer, the elegant mansion that is Stanmer House, and enough land to provide a park and a future university campus – all for the sum of £225,000. On 1 April 1952 just over 1,000 acres of Stanmer parish, which included the large Coldean estate development, were officially transferred to the county borough of Brighton.

There were also those who wanted to attract industry to the area and those who wanted to prevent this kind of development. The town had already established a reputation for engineering. During the 1910s a small area of diamond and engineering factories developed around the Coombe Road area of the Lewes Road corridor. Now, though the railway works were being run down, up to three thousand people were employed by Allen West Ltd, a firm of electrical engineers with a large base in Moulsecoomb Way, which had made a big contribution to the war effort in the form of radar sets and sections of the Mulberry harbour for the D-Day landings. Further engineering firms were brought into the area when the corporation turned 18 acres of land on the fringe of the Downs into the Hollingbury industrial estate.

The Hollingbury industrial estate today (or tonight)

In the development plan, however, only 150 acres of downland were reserved for industry. The planners were, at least, determined to preserve the surrounding Downs as a green belt for the citizens of Brighton. So the war between the forces of change and conservation focused on the town itself. Although St Margaret's church was demolished in 1959, the 1950s were largely times of triumph for the Regency Society. Stanmer House and Patcham Court farmhouse and barn were saved from demolition, and in 1957 the Historic Buildings Council recommended an annual block grant for the restoration of important groups of buildings in Brighton – with the proviso that the corporation should make an equivalent grant.

Another of the Regency Society's aims was to 'ensure that old buildings are not wantonly destroyed and that if replanning is essential new buildings should harmonize with the old'. Here, it clearly failed during the Swinging Sixties. But what chance did it have? If contemporary developers had any aesthetic sensibility, it appears to have evaporated with the fabled white heat of the times. To quote a Saturday morning market stallholder, 'they've pulled a lot of properties down – and put up monstrosities'. Fashionable architectural theory combined with sometimes laudable motives to produce such monstrosities. Some of the so-called 'slums', for example, had been damaged during the war and redevelopment had

The Bedford Hotel before . . .

. . . and after

Churchill Square: white
elephant?

been delayed by post-war shortages. Now, the miracle cure for the housing shortage was the high-rise block. The first tower-blocks were built on Albion Hill in 1961, and others soon followed. One of the ugliest must be the Bedford Towers monolith built on the site of the illustrious hotel, which burned to the ground on 1 April 1964.

Like many other places, Brighton felt it needed a modern shopping centre befitting a brave new world. Thus Churchill Square was created. One might forgive it as a brave failure, were it not for the temerity of the planners. The scheme involved wholesale demolition of a 16 acre site, which included the Grand Hotel. It was, the proponents claimed, 'the key to Brighton's future', 'an effort to create a new Brighton in a contemporary idiom' and dissenting voices were dismissed as 'sterile opposition'. The Grand was not replaced by an amusement centre; it was listed by the government and thereby saved, but an article by Pat Moorman in the *Brighton & Hove Leader* of 12 August 1993 reminisces on 'the quaint little streets that used to lead up from the beach to Western Road. Lined with cottages and shops, many of them cobble-stoned, they were a delight that would today rival The Lanes as a tourist attraction.'

In their place, residents and holidaymakers were bequeathed the Kingswest Centre, a series of multi-storey car parks, an eighteen-storey tower block and Churchill Square itself, a windswept concrete plain on two levels with seventy shop premises and 105,000 sq. ft of office space. Opened in October 1968 at a cost of £9 million, Churchill Square is already outmoded: shoppers now demand heated indoor emporia on the scale of the Metro Centre, Gateshead or Meadowhall, Sheffield. Already there is talk of major cosmetic surgery, even demolition.

The Spa's spared façade now shelters a nursery school

Other, arguably insensitive developments of the time include the redevelopment of the Edward Street/Eastern Road area, which featured a plethora of tower blocks, a dual carriageway, the John Street police station, the law courts and DSS offices. Despite its Grade II listing, Thomas Attree's resplendent Italianate villa, which once graced the northern edge of Queen's Park, was demolished in 1971. But perhaps the most futile act of destruction was committed that same year, when the town's only major Regency Gothic building, the Central National School in Church Street, was demolished while a protection order was delayed by a postal strike. As often, the culprit was the motor car: the building was pulled down in the name of road-widening. But the road has never been widened.

There were, however, some victories in the name of conservation. A car park planned for the Regency Square lawns was finally built underground. The Royal Spa building in Queen's Park was spared from the bulldozers. A scheme to replace Mrs Fitzherbert's former home, Steine House, with an office block was defeated and it is now used as a YMCA hostel. The town's only remaining almshouses, which stand at the foot of Elm Grove, were once earmarked for demolition, but are now listed and restored. Indeed, the whole Hanover area was designated a 'general improvement area' from 1969–76, and thereby escaped the fate of neighbouring Albion and Carlton Hills. The safety of the Downs was reinforced in 1966 when they were designated both an Area of Outstanding Natural Beauty (AONB) and an Environmentally Sensitive Area (ESA).

In 1970 Brighton's favourite resident thespian, Lord Olivier, led a successful protest against the demise of kipper breakfasts on the 'Brighton Belle'. Three years later British Rail was caught up in another storm of protest when it revealed plans to rebuild Brighton station. That same year the building was listed – and the Brighton Society came into being to add muscle to the fight for conservation. The product of a time when 'modern' meant 'progressive', the society values 'the individual character of local streets and neighbourhoods' and seeks to preserve a quality hitherto 'easily destroyed by haphazard demolition and unsympathetic "improvements"'.

Not all of the era's legacies bear the hallmark of philistinism. A campus for the new University of Sussex – the first of a new generation of red-brick universities, granted its royal charter in 1961 – was designed by Sir Basil Spence, and constructed during the 1960s on a 160 acre site in Stanmer Park with scarcely the loss of a single tree. In 1970 a polytechnic (now University of Brighton) was created. With a large college of technology already established, further and higher education came to play an increasingly prominent role in the life of the town. Today, Brighton's population includes around eighteen thousand full-time students. Mainly during the summer months, the student population is swollen by up to fifty thousand foreign students, who come for the summer camps or to learn English at the thirty or so official language schools. Education is now the largest single employment sector in Brighton.

The influx of students also accelerated the boom in youth culture. Boutiques began to spring up in the Lanes; for a time, the Hippodrome and the Regent became rock music venues. The new university quickly acquired a reputation for political activism and 'moral laxity'. During the efflorescence of 'flower power', Dr Josephine Klein, a sociology

Brighton Marina: the complex
takes shape

lecturer, was granted the use of Archway 167 on the lower esplanade
for the study of beatniks, hippies and other young people 'who
generally wish to opt out of conventional society'. It soon provoked
another public protest, and Archway 167 was closed down in 1967.

Brighton acquired a new image as a young persons' town. In some
ways, the energy of youth culture has helped to counteract south
coast atrophy. In other ways, the energy has had a detrimental effect.
Walking down East Street one day in the late 1970s, I stumbled upon
a riot of rampaging mods in parkas, apparently re-enacting a scene
from fifteen years back. In fact, they were shooting *Quadrophenia*
that day: a film dramatizing the rivalry between mods and rockers
which culminated in the notorious pitched battles over the Whitsun
bank holiday weekend of 1964. With the help of 'PC Rain', 150
police managed to quell the fracas, but bank holiday violence
became, for a while, a part of youth culture.

The bad publicity it brought Brighton did nothing for the family
holiday trade. By then, however, the tourist industry appeared to be
wasting away. By the early 1970s it had reached a nadir: there was
no summer show, the Hippodrome had closed and the Palace Pier
theatre had collapsed. The West Pier closed completely at the end of
September 1975. Literally and metaphorically, the paint was peeling
all over Brighton. It was clear that the town had to invest,
substantially, to secure its own future.

The first Brighton Festival of the Arts, held in 1967, had incurred a
loss. Despite the council's annual financial commitment, it was some
time before the festival established itself and secured Brighton's
reputation as a cultural centre. Other ways of bringing in visitors had
to be considered. The biggest, riskiest and most controversial scheme
was to be the Marina. Successive plans to provide Brighton with a

harbour had been aborted throughout the previous century. In 1963 a £9 million plan was proposed to build a three thousand berth harbour, along with flats, houses, a cinema, theatre, casino, car parks and hovercraft and helicopter stations. Today, after years of public debate and escalating costs, after the opening and closure, one year later, of a jetfoil service to Dieppe, the £41 million complex is still not complete. But Brighton has a monumental harbour, a waterside village, a superstore, a six-screen cinema complex and one of the largest artificial yacht marinas in the world. Moreover, Sir John Betjeman's nightmare of 'another Costa del Sol or Benidorm' has not transpired.

A more immediate pay-off came from the Conference Centre. The town's conference tradition goes back to the mid-nineteenth century, when the Pavilion was put to civic use by its new owners. By the early 1970s demand had outgrown its replacement, the Dome. In the face of competition from Blackpool's new facilities, and under the driving force of Tony Hewison, the director of the Resort and Conferences Department, the council unveiled plans for a purpose-built centre. When James Callaghan, the prime minister of the time, formally opened the Conference Centre on 19 September 1977, the planned £3 million investment had tripled. The rather dour grey concrete building has not pleased everyone, but the Brighton Centre was then the largest building of its kind, equipped to seat 5,000

The late lamented Palladium: one of the prices to pay for a lucrative Conference Centre

delegates in its main auditorium, 1,200 in its banqueting suite and a further 800 in a smaller, adjacent hall. Despite subsequent competition from Bournemouth, Harrogate and now Birmingham, the centre has been in continuous use since 1977: not only as a centre for major political party conferences and minor miscellaneous events like conventions for aerobics, barbershop singers and Star Trekkers, but also as a venue for music concerts, tennis tournaments and, during the summer of 1993, a dinosaur exhibition. Though the Birmingham Centre was part-funded by both the government and the EC, Brighton had to foot its entire bill. The council's faith in its own town has reaped handsome dividends: around 1,500 conferences each year contribute some £60 million to the local economy – almost half the income derived from the traditional cash cow, tourism.

Moreover, both the Brighton Centre and the Metropole's lavish Exhibition Halls have boosted the hotel trade. Without this injection, the £10 million refurbishment of the Grand Hotel, following the IRA bomb of 12 October 1984, might never have been contemplated. Without it, would approval have been given for the £12 million improvement of the Metropole and the £25 million investment in the Ramada Renaissance hotel? True, the latter was to destroy part of the ancient street pattern of the Old Town, but it was voted one of the top three new hotels in Europe. Renamed the Hospitality Inn in 1989, the hotel, like the Grand, now boasts five-star status.

Given the monied visitors which these hotels now cater for, preservation of Brighton's heritage, its unique selling point, became yet more imperative. A major survey of tourism in 1984 reinforced the need for 'conservation of Brighton's environment'. The Royal Pavilion, in particular, became a focus for major investment. Following the post-war Regency Exhibitions, the queen returned many of the original pieces of furniture, and its popularity peaked at around four hundred thousand visitors per annum during the 1960s and early '70s. Notwithstanding the virtual destruction of the Music Room by an arsonist in 1975, the nocturnal floodlights, which bathed the fibre-glass minarets in shades of Edinburgh Rock, seemed to proclaim its born-again pre-eminence. Then the lights went out. For years, the Pavilion was cocooned in blue plastic while a massive programme of painstaking restoration was undertaken. Even the artificial minarets were replaced by genuine Bath stone. In the summer of 1990 the massive scaffolding structure and the blue wraps were taken down to reveal an exterior restored to its former glory. Inside, the results of the £10 million investment were revealed gradually over the next few years. Now, three hundred thousand or more visitors generate an annual income of well over £1 million.

North Laine housing. What a little care and conservation can do

Only a quarter of the money came from English Heritage grants. Once more, the rest has had to be found by Brighton's rate-payers. Remember, too, that this investment was embarked upon during a recession which created widespread redundancies and rising unemployment as one after another of the town's engineering firms closed down. The national economy during the 1980s and '90s has been on a roller-coaster ride, with upturns following and preceding downturns. Fortunately, the slump in engineering has been partly offset by a boom in financial services, with first American Express, then Trustcard and Lloyds Bank's International Factors all establishing major centres in the town. But one of the more obvious victims of recession has been the West Pier. While the sea front has been enlivened during the time by the opening of Brighton's controversial nudist beach, the marooning of the Greek cargo ship, *The Athina B*, and the rebirth of the Palace Pier, the saga of the West Pier has run and run. The forces of conservation and change became locked in a stalemate as English Heritage withdrew its promised grants in the face of a proposed £30 million rebuilding scheme – already approved by its owners, the West Pier Trust. Now, the old pier has been cast adrift from the esplanade; the money is no longer there for a refit. It is a cruel irony that its brasher sister is thriving on the millions of pounds invested by its owners, the Noble Organization. With around three-and-a-half million visitors every year, the Palace Pier is now the fifth most popular tourist attraction in Britain.

For a council burdened by major investment programmes, recession has also meant less money to invest in housing. Rebuilding of the troubled Whitehawk estate was already under way, but the need to address 'Bedsit Land' was equally pressing. A look at the electoral rolls shows how Sussex Square, for instance, originally mansion houses owned by lords, ladies and knights of the realm, has been divided and sub-divided: Nos 39 and 40 now list twenty-one flats and thirty-two voters. Sussex Square, however, is in a much better state of repair than, say, Brunswick Terrace. The temptation for wholesale redevelopment must have been as strong as it was in the immediate post-war years.

There are a number of reasons why this nightmare hasn't transpired. Strangely, recession has saved some vulnerable properties. With the boom and subsequent crash in property prices, the value of the site itself outweighed the value of the existing or planned property. Where developers have gone bankrupt, the council has been able to refurbish the existing property or gain a bigger say in how the site should be developed. As in the days when the Old Town was hemmed in by agriculture, land for development is scarce. Moreover, the council itself is by far the biggest owner of land in Brighton and, obviously, has a vested interest in what happens on its sites. Faced with bankruptcy itself, however, it needs to generate revenue. Nevertheless, ever since the council rejected the 'Wilson Report' of 1973, which threatened the North Laine with 'spine-roads' and car parks, there has been evidence of a more responsible attitude. North Laine and nine other districts have been designated as town centre conservation areas, there is a new chief planning officer and 'green' issues are generally now coming higher up the agenda.

True, the redevelopment of Bartholomew Square and West Street are open to criticism, but Dukes Lane and the Jew Street Media Centre have been unqualified successes. There is enough to suggest that the Regency and Brighton Societies and, since 1982, the Lewis Cohen Urban Studies Centre at the University of Brighton, have done much to change attitudes. There is still more to be done: the 'freeze the breeze' campaign is fighting for more emphasis on public transport to ease town centre traffic congestion and counteract a car-oriented 'breeze into Brighton' message; there is a need for more low-cost housing like the Tichborne Street development and fewer office premises like the Brighton Station complex. Battles have been won, but the war is not over. Nevertheless, the Brighton Society's aim of achieving that 'proper balance', with 'constructive consultation' addressing 'social needs as well as . . . commercial factors' and paying 'respect . . . to the existing surroundings' no longer looks like so much pie in the sky. The debate over how the Jubilee Street site should be developed has been so protracted precisely because the large-scale option is not now the only one: a much smaller scale

'Kill the atmosphere means kill the trees.' Another victim of the hurricane.

mixed development of houses, shops and workshops is mooted – one more in keeping with the North Laine community ambience.

The balance is a very delicate one. During the night of Friday 16 October 1987 that balance might have been permanently upset by the force of nature. Winds of more than 100 m.p.h. ripped through the town and across the whole south coast. A 2 ton minaret crashed through the roof of the recently restored Music Room of the Royal Pavilion and embedded itself in the new £86,000 carpet; mercifully, it missed a load-bearing beam by a matter of inches. Walls were shattered, roofs were wrecked, cars were overturned, beach huts were bowled along the esplanade and caravans were splintered. They could all be repaired. The loss of over two thousand five hundred mature trees, however, has permanently disfigured Brighton's landscape. The violence of the hurricane recalled the great storms of 1703 and 1705, and served as an unsolicited reminder that developers, councillors and conservationists are not alone in dictating the destiny of Brighton.

CHAPTER NINE

Days of Future Past

We should not fool ourselves into thinking we are in total control of what comes next.

from *A Quality Future: An Economic Strategy for East Sussex*
(1991)

uring my research for this book, I asked a number of people what they thought Brighton would be like in the year 2000. No one could see it changing much. Someone told me confidently, 'It will survive'.

One thing, I believe, is certain: Brighton *will* change. Its history confirms that. It also confirms another certainty:

A restored Pavilion and its nearly restored grounds

Underneath the arches . . . a
new museum

that it will surely adapt to whatever changes are in the offing. The East
Sussex Tourism Strategy, *A Quality Experience*, suggests a number of
imminent challenges for the future. There will be competition from
major tourist developments such as theme parks; there are the effects
of the Channel Tunnel and the Single European Market to gauge; and
there are major curbs on public spending to face.

Precisely how Brighton will change in response to these
challenges is a matter of conjecture. But there is another likely factor
to the equation: the change won't be as total as it was, say, in the
Victorian era. The lack of public money must dictate that any
changes will be of a piecemeal nature and founded on a partnership
between the private and public sectors. Take the restoration of the
Pavilion grounds to Nash's plans of 1820. The number of partners
contributing to the replanting alone suggests a protracted process of
planning and negotiations: the Ernest Kleinworth Charitable Trust,
the Esmée Fairbairn Charitable Trust, the Priory Charitable Trust,
the John Coates Charitable Trust, the Friends of the Royal Pavilion,
Art Gallery and Museums and, hopefully, English Heritage.

Official plans for change are, on paper at least, reassuring. There
is a healthy emphasis on quality of life, preservation of the past,
protection of the environment, consultation and balance. The
Borough Plan, *Brighton Towards 2000*, sets down the challenge
ahead: that of how to encourage development which will meet local
and housing needs while constrained by the town's physical situation
and historic character. It recognizes that Brighton's historical and
physical legacy 'attracts the many thousands of visitors upon whom
the prosperity of Brighton . . . depends', but equally 'it is prosperity

Sunday morning at the station
market. Note the new office
complex

Protecting its famous coastline

which generates the private and public investment necessary to conserve and improve the historic buildings and spaces within the town'. To rest on its laurels, in other words, would be a recipe for stagnation and decline. The message, according to the Quality Future document, is one of 'economic health with environmental safeguards –"sustainable development"'.

The same document recognizes Brighton as a town of 'unique character'. 'We should cherish the difference,' it proclaims. Certain 'sustainable developments' have taken or will soon take place, which cherish that difference and build on the legacy of the past. The town, remember, grew up as a fishing community. Now that the industry's decline is almost complete, there are plans to turn the arches opposite the Fish Market Hard into a fishing museum. And the Marina's continued growth now reflects Brighton's erstwhile importance as a port. Indeed, there is a cross-Channel service once more: by catamaran, to Fécamp – though currently during the summer months only. A market culture, dating back to the medieval charter, lives on in an abundance of antique shops and open-air markets, which help to bring in and bring back the visitors. Until plans to develop the vacant station site are finalized, Sunday morning bargain-hunters congregate there for the giant weekly car boot sale.

In the eighteenth century Brighton's prosperity was founded when people discovered that the sea offered more than fish. Today, the purity of the English Channel is questionable. However, Southern Water plans to invest £30 million in improving the sewage system, which should help the county council meet its priority target of EC

'Blue Flag' status for all its beaches along the coast. Meanwhile, the borough council continues to invest in protecting its famous coastline from the ravages of its most prized natural asset.

There are signs that British families are thinking more now of a traditional holiday by the sea. A devalued currency and bad publicity surrounding airline strikes are taking their toll on the continental holiday market. The 1992–3 annual report of the English Tourist Board stressed how investment in a quality seaside experience will help to supplant the tired old 'kiss-me-quick' image and attract more family parties to England's resorts. Brighton's £1.5 million investment in a Sea Life Centre to replace the anachronistic Dolphinarium is already beginning to pay dividends. The council now proposes to invest a similar figure in regenerating the sea front: extending facilities along the lower esplanade by offering seedcorn money to attract private investment with a view to improving the quality of the various bars and cafes and making better use of the arches under King's Road. The vision is that of creating a 'string of pearls' which will link a thriving Palace Pier to its revitalized twin and beyond. Perhaps the decking of the West Pier may yet clatter once more with the sound of promenading feet.

The county council's strategic priority for tourism is to 'target the key growth markets of overseas visitors and domestic short breaks, while retaining the traditional British day visitor and main holiday markets'. Though 1992 was a bad year for Brighton, investment and marketing have generated more enquiries for brochures and a higher rate of conversion into hard bookings (62 per cent). Of course, Brighton is not a traditional kind of resort. The beach (such as it is!) does not feature prominently in its marketing; rather, the cosmopolitan shops, the nightlife, special events and good quality accommodation are highlighted to tempt the short-break visitor. And its regular occupancy survey of local hotels shows that levels are lower during the customary peak months of July and August than they are in June, say, or September. Moreover, the town has more all-year-round business than other resorts. Spring and autumn are peak times for conferences and short breaks; there is regular business from Gatwick airport; and during the winter the financial services sector tends to make use of the hotels for functions and training. The town's marketing has also helped to create a strong foothold in western Europe and forge links with Japan, for example. These days, Brighton's hotels regularly cater for travel-trade visits from countries seeking to develop their own tourist industries. Brighton is now the most popular port of call outside London for Saudi Arabian visitors – who spend more per person than anyone else.

So, the prognosis for 'sustainable development' of tourism looks good, especially now that the council's faith in its annual festival of the arts is restoring an image created by George, Prince of Wales: Brighton, centre of arts and culture. Back in the 1920s, an annual carnival was held for two successive years over a four-day period in June. According to the author of *Two Days in Brighton* (1925), it was designed to make Brighton 'better known to visitors from all parts of the country', but it was abandoned after 1923 due to the 'boisterous conduct of the crowd'. Though still aiming for publicity and visitors, the Brighton Festival was a more highbrow affair than its rumbustious predecessor. Indeed, under its first artistic director, it was perceived as rather élitist. Its current artistic director, Gavin Henderson, organized an alternative festival, which focused more on the local artistic community. Since his succession in 1984, the official festival has grown into the largest of its kind in England. Described by a former committee member as 'three weeks and four weekends of artistic indigestion each May', Brighton Festival is now a multi-media extravaganza which pursues the twin aims of developing indigenous work and talent, and fostering greater international involvement and cooperation.

BRIGHTON FESTIVAL

7 - 30 MAY 1993

PROGRAMME

The Brighton Festival: artistic indigestion each May?

Having left the town, I am perhaps more susceptible to its impact. Its broad base is evident both in the quality, say, of the museum's exhibitions and the range of community-based activities. The custom of 'bending in' or blessing the fishing nets and boats has been revived at the beginning of the festival, and the number of special walks and guided tours suggests a popular interest in the town's past. Now, too, many of the town's restaurants have spilled on to streets enlivened by jugglers, buskers and assorted artistes. It seems that, as one shop closes, another arty emporium opens. Today, there is a Latin American shop, a French shop, even a vegetarian shoe shop in the North Laine. Brighton's compact centre has an ambience, these days, of Montmartre-sur-Mer.

The festival has helped the Theatre Royal survive the recessions, and there is talk of new auditoria. The Palace Pier already provides a stage for performance artists, and there are plans to extend it and build a new theatre to seat one thousand five hundred. And if the Top Rank bingo hall in North Street is converted back to the theatre it was when it opened in 1940 (as the Imperial), this could provide another venue for Glyndebourne opera productions.

And the festival has provided an umbrella for local artistic activity. The Dance Agency and the Comedy Festival have grown up under its wing and set up on their own. In 1993 local artists got together and put on an exhibition at the marina. The Media Centre in Jew Street has opened recently to encourage growth of media industries in the area. Brighton has long been a popular location for film crews; maybe more film crews in the future will be home-grown.

Not every legacy has served as a positive foundation for development. Housing and unemployment problems remain to haunt the town's guardians. The *Planning and Development Handbook* estimates that the 'shortfall between the number of people in the town who do and will need a home and the number of homes that currently exist is . . . in excess of 3,500'. The council has initiated the Brighton Housing Forum so that all the agencies responsible for providing housing can work in partnership to ensure that any new housing meets priority needs.

Unemployment has, of course, driven down labour costs and, ironically, cheap labour helped to attract International Factors to Brighton from London. However, the growth in the financial services sector has only partially offset the erosion of Brighton's traditional manufacturing base. There are, as a consequence, existing industrial sites available at Hollingbury, Bevendean and Freshfield Industrial Estates. But the East Sussex economy is based very much on small firms. Education is the town's principal source of employment and Brighton's economic strategy for the next century rests firmly on exploiting the so-called A27 'Academic Corridor':

Restaurants have spilled on to the streets

attracting new high-technology and research-related enterprises linked to the two universities and their human and physical resources. A 'Silicone Valley' in Sussex?

The success of such a strategy is partly dependent on communications. The planning brochures emphasize the need to tackle the town's traffic problem and improve the links by road and rail to London, and to towns along the South Coast. They also press for retention and improvement of the threatened Newhaven to Dieppe link to the continent. Ironically, the imminent completion of the by-pass has created another challenge: that of controlling the development of giant out-of-town supermarkets and shopping complexes. Yes, they provide employment, but they also threaten the town's own shopping centre, a vital ingredient in the recipe to attract visitors.

As to who is to implement these plans to meet the challenge of the coming century, this too is a matter of some speculation. Once again, the prospect of creating one municipal body from the parts of Brighton and Hove raises its chimerical head as one of four proposed options due to be decided in 1994. The other three are Brighton as it is now, a Greater Brighton incorporating Peacehaven and the Adur Council, and a Greater Greater Brighton which would also incorporate Lewes.

The by-pass has improved Brighton's road links, but . . .

The end of the End of the
Pier Show? Not bloomin'
likely!

A special 1904 edition of the *Brighton Gazette* to celebrate fifty
years of municipal government reported how the mayor concluded his
speech 'by expressing the hope that Brighton would always remain
what she was now – the Queen of Watering Places and London-by-the-
Sea'. Brighton is bound to change – and by the year 2000, Hove may
be annexed, the Marina may be finished and the West Pier might even
be restored to former glories – but the Bronze Age discoveries during
the by-pass excavations only go to show that you can't bury your past,
that a town's future is inextricably linked to and, therefore, dependent
on the legacy of the past. So long as the new borough's elected officials
remember this, then she will remain what she is now and was then: a
right royal resort. The indefinable spirit of Brighton will surely flourish
and that heady brew will continue to intoxicate.

Introduction

The two walks I have planned are deliberately contrasting. The first concentrates primarily on the more obvious attractions of Brighton's grand theatrical stage; the second, so to speak, takes you behind the scenes.

Both walks are quite demanding. In both cases, however, it's possible to complete the walk in under two hours. In the summer, there will be more distractions which might prolong the tours. It could be sensible to start with a visit to the Tourist Information Centre (opposite the town hall in Bartholomew Square) in order to check on things like opening times. I would also suggest a visit to the travel information hut on the Old Steine (opposite the Royal York buildings). A bus timetable would be useful in the event of failing feet.

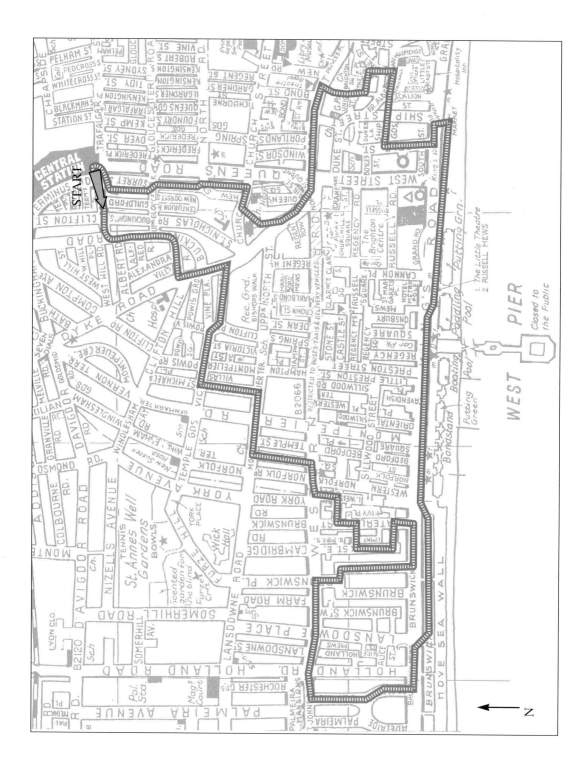

1: Brighton Station Circular

This walk focuses partly on the splendours of the sea front west of the Palace Pier, and partly on the 'twittens' and other less explored byways which lead you down from and back to the station. The Lanes and the front itself can be thronging with people at most hours of the day; for this reason, an early morning (8.30 a.m.) or, in summer, a mid-afternoon (4.00) start would be my preference. The walk is about 3 miles long and should take 1½ to 2 hours to complete.

After admiring the iron work of H.E. Wallis's superb arched roof, **emerge from the station, turn right, cross over Terminus Road at the traffic lights and start walking up Guildford Road.**

Cross over Guildford Road and walk down Camden Terrace. Cross Upper Gloucester Road at a slight angle to your left. **Walk down North Gardens.** Notice the charming Regency cottages behind their gardens. Then **cross over North Road and walk down Crown Gardens.** The bow-windowed cottages date from the 1820s, and were reputedly built for employees of the Royal Pavilion and stables.

You will emerge from Crown Gardens opposite a new building erected on the site of the old Sussex Throat and Ear Hospital. **Turn right and head up Church Street to St Nicholas's church.** Turn round before you enter the churchyard: there is a good view of Amex House and the Edward Street redevelopment. In the churchyard, look out for the graves of Amon Wilds (down to the left), Martha Gunn and Phoebe Hessel (just by the path), and Nicholas Tettersell. If time permits, look inside the church and find the Norman font. **Follow the path out of the churchyard and head down towards the clock tower.** On your left are the Regency Gothic houses of Wykeham Terrace. No. 7 was the home of Dame Flora Robson; Nos 1–5 and 8–11 formed part of St Mary's Home (for female penitents).

At the clock tower, **cross over Queen's Road to Boots** (built on the site of the old Regent cinema). Then **head down North Street,** past the Top Rank bingo hall, once the Imperial Theatre and then the Essoldo cinema. **Cross over the road opposite Vokins.** Further down North Street, **turn right into Meeting House Lane** (said to be haunted by the ghost of a walled-up nun). **Follow this lane** on its serpentine route **to Brighton Place** (perhaps taking a slight detour to look at Brighton Square, one of the more successful redevelopments of the 1960s). This is the area once known as The Knab.

Turn right in the direction of the town hall and the new Bartholomew Square development, **then right up Prince Albert Street. Cross over the road** towards the Cricketers Arms and the Black Lion (a reconstruction of the brewery founded by Deryk Carver). **Head down Black Lion Lane** between the two, past the venerable listed cottages, the oldest in the Old Town. **Cross over Ship Street and head down Ship Street Gardens**, once, reputedly, the main rope-making area of Brighton.

You will emerge at Middle Street. Just round to the right is the Hippodrome. **Turn left and follow the street down to the front**, passing the Byzantine-style Brighton Synagogue on your left. **Cross over King's Road by the lights to your left, then head down to the lower esplanade.**

Walk along the esplanade for a couple of hundred yards. You will pass the new Fish Market Hard on your left and the arches which are to be refurbished as a fishing museum on your right. **Climb back up the steps** to the site of the old West Battery on King's Road for a look at the Grand and Metropole Hotels. Back towards the Palace Pier are the Brighton Centre and Kingswest Boulevard.

Walk along the front for a further half mile or so. You will pass the West Pier and, across the road, Regency Square, built on the Belle Vue Field and the first Brighton Military Camp. Further along to your right are the new Bedford Hotel and Bedford Square (right opposite the 'birdcage' bandstand). Once you pass the Norfolk Hotel and reach the Peace Memorial, you are standing on the threshold of Hove. Across the road is Embassy Court.

Cross the invisible boundary into Hove and continue as far as Adelaide Crescent by way of the esplanade, Brunswick Lawns or either side of Kingsway, being sure to admire first Brunswick Terrace and Square. **Cross the main road** by the most convenient lights and **climb the ornamental steps up to Adelaide Crescent**. By walking up the east side towards Palmeira Square, you will pass the ten original houses built in 1830 to the design of Decimus Burton. Those built twenty years later have much plainer facades.

Turn right at the north-east corner of Palmeira Square, cross over Holland Road and walk along Western Road as far as Brunswick Place. Then head down the eastern side of Brunswick Square and back to Kingsway. Turn left and walk along to Waterloo Street. Just across the street is Charles Barry's chapel for the Brunswick estate, St Andrew's church. Have a look down the passage beside it at Chapel Mews; the weather-beaten rear elevation of Embassy Court looms above. **Cross back over Waterloo Street and wander into Brunswick Street East** for a look at the backs of the houses of the Square and some of the mews houses of the original estate. **Find your way back to Waterloo Street** via the dilapidated original market building and through the ceremonial arch.

Cross over Waterloo Street again, walk up towards Western Road, then turn right into Cross Street. Turn up Little Western Road, cross over the road for a look at the boundary stone in the pavement. Walk back towards Brighton, then turn up Borough Street, which commemorates the creation of the parliamentary borough in 1832. The bow-fronted terraced houses are delightful.

At the top of Borough Street, **turn right into Montpelier Place**. Opposite is St Stephen's church and a favourite haunt, The Little Bookshop. **Cross over Montpelier Road and turn up Montpelier Villas** for a look at some of Amon Henry Wilds's finest works. This is the heart of the Clifton area. **Turn right at the top** into Victoria Road. St Michael's church is opposite. Built in the Gothic revival style, the stained glass is by Rossetti and William Morris. **Follow Victoria Road to Clifton Terrace**, the last of Brighton's Regency treasures. **Walk along the raised pavement to Dyke Road.**

Walk up Dyke Road as far as the Royal Alexandra Hospital. Cross over the road and head down Leopold Road. This West Hill area was built on the grounds of the old workhouse. **Walk**

along Buckingham Road: No. 31 was the birthplace of Aubrey Beardsley. **Turn down Guildford Road and back to the station**. This time, take in David Mocatta's Italianate design (plus subsequent embellishments).

2: Palace Pier Circular

This isn't an easy walk! It's uphill all the way to the top of Queen's Park, but there are some good views and the second half is 'plain sailing'. It'll give you a good idea of Brighton's topography and the town's artisan hinterland. There are some interesting churches (and shops) en route, and because the main body of the walk is off the track usually beaten by tourists, it doesn't matter too much which time of day you choose. The distance is about 3 miles and should take about 2 hours.

In summer, **start by taking Volk's railway as far as the Marina station. Walk back towards the Palace Pier for about 100 yd, cross over the road and walk up the Kemp Town slope to Marine Parade**. Lewes Crescent will be in front of you. To your left is the summit of Duke's Mound which leads back down to Madeira Drive. It was named after the Duke of Devonshire, who lived at No. 1 (and No. 14 Arundel Terrace) at the south-east corner of the Crescent. It was later the home of Edward VII's daughter, Princess Louise. The Crescent spans 840 ft between Arundel Terrace and Chichester Terrace on the west.

In winter, catch one of the buses that stops on Marine Parade opposite the Sea Life Centre and get off as near to Lewes Crescent as possible.

Walk back towards the pier along Marine Parade. Note (among other things) the fine canopy next to Belgrave House, the beautiful iron work of Bristol Court and the columns of Portland Place. Marine Square was built between 1823 and 1825 for the famous solicitor, Thomas Attree. It is probably the work of Wilds and Busby. No. 11 was once the home of Cardinal Newman.

In summer, **use the Madeira Lift for a quick look at the Shelter Hall** as it is today. Then **continue down Marine Parade**, past Bloomsbury Place, a fairly typical side street of the East Cliff. The bow fronts and iron balconies allowed views of the sea. Rufford

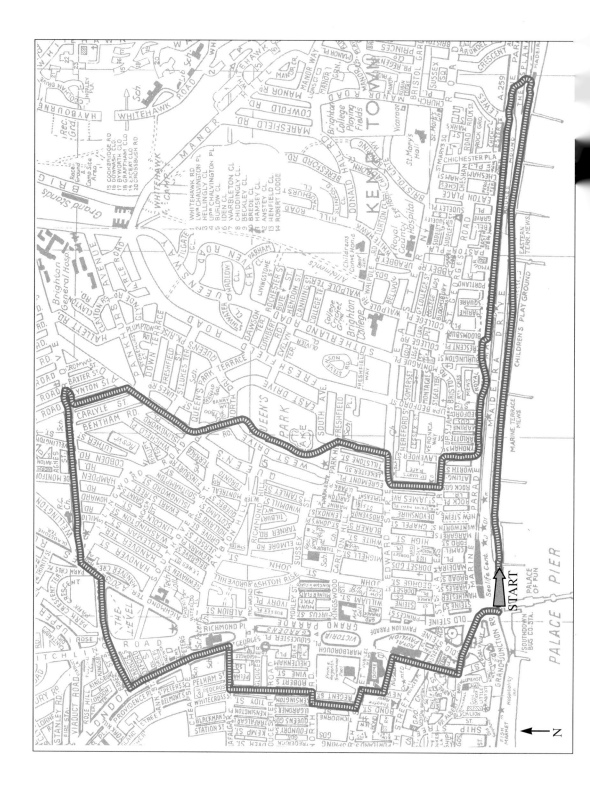

Court on the corner of Crescent Place is a fairly extraordinary construction, well worth a look. No. 25 Burlington Street was the home of Max Miller. **Cross over near here for a closer look at Royal Crescent.**

Continue back towards the Palace Pier. As you cross Bedford Street, Terence Rattigan's former house is on the corner. **Turn up Grafton Street**: the tall bow-fronted early nineteenth-century houses are listed. **Turn left into St James's Street and cross over the road** for a look at St Mary's church, rebuilt in French Gothic style when part of the original classical building (by A.H. Wilds) collapsed.

Turn right up Upper Rock Gardens to the lights at Eastern Road. Cross over and head to the right as far as Park Street. Turn up Park Street and head for the entrance arch into Queen's Park. Note the cobble-fronted cottages dating from the 1820s on your left; the old slipper baths on your right have now been pulled down for the redevelopments.

Go into the park and head north-west towards the 'Pepper-Pot' (slightly left of straight ahead!) by meandering through the middle or skirting the left-hand side of the park. The leaking lake has recently been repaired; it was once used as a roller-skating rink. Note the remains of the Royal Spa in the south-west corner behind you: it is now part of a nursery school. At the top of the park, **cross over to Tower Road**: the 'Pepper-Pot' is straight ahead. This stood once in the grounds of the Italianate villa designed by Sir Charles Barry for Thomas Attree, who bought the park in the 1820s. The 'Pepper-Pot' may have been a water or observation tower for the villa; it was used as the latter during the Second World War.

Turn right up Queen's Park Road. You will pass St Luke's church on your right. Look up the side street by Queen's Park Tavern to see the stand of the racecourse. **Cross over the road and walk down Arnold Street,** typical of the densely-populated Hanover district – which escaped the post-war bulldozers. You will come out **at Elm Grove**, the main road from town to the racecourse. Just up the hill to your right is Brighton General Hospital, once the workhouse. **Cross diagonally over to the right** to see how St Wilfrid's, a 1930s church much admired by Sir John Betjeman, has been converted into sheltered housing.

WALKING
TOUR

Walking **down Elm Grove** will give you a good idea of the lie of the land. You will be able to see St Bartholomew's church rising above the shops of the London Road area. The church at the bottom right is the Catholic church of St Joseph's. **Cross over Elm Grove and walk down past the Percy and Wagner Almshouses.** These Gothic revival houses were built in 1795. They were saved from demolition during the 1960s and restored in 1975–6. Before you cross over to the Level, take a look at A.H. Wilds's Hanover Crescent. No. 11 was the home of Sir Rowland Hill – of penny post and LBSC railway fame.

Cross over the Lewes Road to the Level and walk along its northern perimeter (Union Road). Once an area of swampy ground where the intermittent streams from the London and Lewes Road valleys converged, it became and remains a popular recreational site. The wall to the right encloses the private garden of Park Crescent. This was originally an esteemed cricket ground (and probably the first county cricket ground in the land) and part of the Royal Gardens. The avenues of great elms sadly were ravaged by the 1987 hurricane.

If you're out on a weekday, **cross over the road and walk through the Open Market to the London Road.** Alternatively, walk down Oxford Street. Now you will be able to appreciate the full majesty of St Bart's. **Turn left, walk down the London Road for a few yards and cross over at the controlled crossing. Turn left again and walk in the direction of the sea.** As you pass St Peter's church on your left, **turn up Trafalgar Street to the right.** This is the North Laine area. Brighton station is at the top of the road.

Pass by the charming Pelham Square on your left and **turn left into Sydney Street. Then cross Gloucester Road diagonally right to Kensington Gardens.** The Cheese Shop is on the left; the original Body Shop a few doors further down. **Cross over North Road, again diagonally right and walk down Gardner Street.** You will come out at North Road. **Cross over the road, turn left and then right into New Road.** A.H. Wilds's classical Unitarian church (said to be modelled on the Temple of Theseus at Athens). Further down on the right is the Theatre Royal and what remains of a colonnade which once extended round the corner into North Street.

Cross over the road just before the theatre and follow the path beside the Dome into the Pavilion grounds. Meander around the

restored pathways, past the Pavilion entrance and out via
the South Gate. You will now be facing Castle Square, once the
commercial and coaching centre of the town. **Cross over by
the lights opposite Hannington's, and walk along East Street as
far as Bartholomews Avenue.** The town hall and the new square are
up to your right. **Cross over East Street, however, and follow the
avenue to the Old Steine.** To your left is Marlborough House, the
oldest remaining house on the Steine and remodelled by Robert
Adam when the Duke of Marlborough sold up in 1786. Beside it is
Steine House, built for Mrs Fitzherbert.

Turn right and follow the Steine past the passageway into Pool
Valley, past one of Sir Harry Preston's former hotels, the Royal York
Buildings, past his other great hotel, the Royal Albion, built on the
site of Dr Russell's house, **back to Grand Junction Road and the
Palace Pier.**

The Next Steps

O ne of the most useful first steps would be a trip to the Tourist Information Centre in Bartholomew Square. Get yourself a map and start exploring!

A visit to the Royal Pavilion is, of course, essential (tel. 0273 603005). I would strongly recommend a visit to Brighton Museum (603005) in Church Street. Anyone interested in doing some further reading would be well advised to visit Brighton Reference Library (691197 or 601197), also in Church Street, and/or the Lewis Cohen Urban Studies Centre (600900) at 68 Grand Parade.

The two best sources I discovered for illustrations and old photographs of Brighton are the Brighton Reference Library and the Postcard Saloon at 36 Queens Road. Copies of the photographs from Robert Jeeves's splendid collection are available for sale in black and white or sepia in a variety of sizes – mounted, framed or simply as cards. The reference library, too, can sell copies of the illustrations and photographs from their collection.

Finally, there are so many good books on Brighton that it is hard to recommend specific volumes. However, the following is a list of those which I found particularly useful or interesting:

Carder, Timothy, *The Encyclopaedia of Brighton* (East Sussex County Libraries, 1990)
Gilbert, Edmund, *Brighton, Old Ocean's Bauble* (Harvester Books, 1974 or Flare Books, 1975)
Musgrave, Clifford, *Life in Brighton* (Faber, 1970)
Dale, Anthony, *About Brighton* (The Regency Society, 1986)
Betjeman, John and Gray, J.S., *Victorian and Edwardian Brighton from Old Photographs* (B.T. Batsford, 1972)
A Guide to the Buildings of Brighton (Brighton Polytechnic, 1987)
The Royal Pavilion Brighton, official guidebook

Many of the oral histories published by QueenSpark Books are fascinating. I referred to:

No. 9, *Hard Times and Easy Terms* (Bert Healey); No. 13, *Who was Harry Cowley?*; No. 20, *Backyard Brighton*; No. 21, *Everything*

Seems Smaller (Sid Manville); No. 22, *Back Street Brighton;* No. 23, *Moulescoomb Days* (Ruby Dunn).

The archaeological and ancient history brochures available from Brighton Museum and the information leaflets published by the Lewis Cohen Urban Studies Centre (and also available from the Tourist Information Centre) are also recommended.

Acknowledgements

My special thanks to Cliff Edwards ('Mr Brighton') for sharing his knowledge, expertise and enthusiasm with a complete stranger; and to Robert Jeeves of the Postcard Saloon for letting me plunder his photographic treasures. Without them both, this book may not have been possible.

My grateful thanks to all of the following for their generous help: Anne Burrill, Hannie Lixenberg and Phil Barnes of the Royal Pavilion; Elaine Jewell and the staff of Brighton Reference Library; Rob Fraser and Kevin Kingston of the Environmental Services Department, Warwick Toone (Tourism Officer), Jackie Lythell and Liz Solkhon, all of Brighton Borough Council; Roger Neil of the Theatre Royal; Jackie Frisby of Brighton Museum; Roger Davey (County Archivist), Dr Andrew Woodcock (County Archaeology Officer) and Sarah Boughton of East Sussex County Council; Selma Montford of the Lewis Cohen Urban Studies Centre; John Denman of the Regency Society; Mrs Card of Sussex Stationers; David Beevers of Preston Manor; Hilary Nelson of Howlett Clarke Cushman, Solicitors; John Heron of Lumiere Pictures; John Funnell, Roger Bamber and Jim Cooke.

Thanks, too, to Tony and Carol, Angie and Chris, Allan and Deborah for the overnight stays; Nigel and Judith for lending me their table for a desk; Louise for lending me her camera.

And last, but far from least, thanks for my daily succour to Harri Hall, my wife, and Stan and Dizzy, my cats.

Picture Credits

The photographs and assorted illustrations on the following pages were reproduced with the kind permission of: front cover and pp. 8, 41 (margin), the Royal Pavilion, Art Gallery and Museums, Brighton; pp. 12 (top), 14, 21, 24, 25, 27, 31, 32, 35, 36, 37, 40, 41 (bottom), 45, 48, 67, 68, 71, 77, 80, Brighton Reference Library; pp. 19 (bottom), 29, 54, 55, 56, 59, 60, 61, 62, 65, 66, 69 (top), 70, 72, 75, 79, 82 (top), 87, Robert Jeeves, The Postcard Saloon; pp. 81, 98, Jim Cooke; pp. viii, 11, 91, 94, Brighton Borough Council, Environmental Services Department; p. 33, Brighton Borough Council, Arts and Leisure Services; p. 9, East Sussex County Council; p. 73, Lumière Pictures Film Library; p. 6 (margin), Roger Bamber; p. 96, Tess Roberts; p. ii, Mrs Whitmore; p. 69 (margin), Theatre Royal, Brighton. The rest of the photographs were taken by the author.

Index

With the exception of specific places or people, this index is arranged, generally, by topics: for example, churches come under religion, the workhouse comes under poverty, etc.